# LETHAL EFFECTS
## OF
# PYSCHOTRAUMA
## VINDICATION OF LOVE AND GRACE

## WILLIE JAMES WEBB

# LETHAL EFFECTS OF PSYCHOTRAUMA

## VINDICATION OF LOVE AND GRACE

WILLIE JAMES WEBB

ISBN: 979-8-9917289-4-2 PB
ISBN: 979-8-9917289-5-9 HB

Printed in the U.S.A

To Wilma and Karen,

Who felt my pain, shared my sorrows, and stood by me during my struggle for human justice.

# TABLE OF CONTENTS

# ACKNOWLEDGEMENTS

It is a time-consuming endeavor to probe deeply into one's heart, mind, and soul and verbally externalize the essence of what is found. It takes substantial thought and energy to examine and select certain life experiences and fashion them into a unified and meaningful expression. The time and energy given to writing Psychotrauma, I am sure, was time and energy taken away from my family. I express my gratitude to my wife, Wilma, and my daughter, Karen, for allowing me the time and the space to do this writing. I am indebted to a long list of people who gave understanding, sympathy and encouragement. I am indebted to the long list of clients who allowed themselves to become vulnerable by baring their souls and entrusting me with their secret thoughts and their private feelings. And if there were those who did not wish me well, God allowed it for some good purpose. I consider myself indebted to them as well, for the lessons, although bitter, that they taught me.

Willie James Webb

# CHAPTER 1

## Introduction

There is a need to express forcefully, that human injustice is a painful, destructive, and lethal social disease. Psychotrauma: The Human Injustice Crisis, is an effort to document the destructive influence of human injustice. There is a direct link between injustice and stress, injustice and violence, injustice and depression. There is a direct link between injustice and homicide, injustice and suicide. The destructive influence of injustice grossly impairs the normal functioning of human individuals. Most significantly, it has been known to transform persons of good moral character into dangerous killers. It is a contagious venomous poison.

Economic deprivation is at the core of the human injustice crisis. Human rights violations involving economic security are the basis of widespread psychotrauma. Injustice aimed at undermining a person's economic security seems to have the greatest effects in triggering psychotrauma. Human rights violations involving job rights and property rights are the most common precipitators of psychotrauma. Job rights and property rights appear to be more essential to the individual psychological well-being than what has been previously acknowledged. To deprive a person of his means of livelihood, unjustly, can mean, to deprive a person of his life.

After a thorough examination of the literature, it is concluded that this work is the most complete and comprehensive account of the destructive process of psychotrauma. It reveals the innermost workings of the brain and the mind under extreme psychological pressure. It describes an overload and breakdown of the mind. It illustrates and demonstrates the meaning of the breaking point. For the first time, human injustice is linked to this destructive process. The relationship between injustice and violence is illustrated and dramatized. Injustice is not a passive, covert, benign act. Injustice is an act of violence with legal and criminal implications.

In spite of the destructive influence of injustice, there is a bright spot and a reason to be hopeful. That hope is based on the fact that with love and justice, many of the damaging effects of injustice are reversible. Love and justice are great forces of balance. Through love and justice, the crooked places can be made straight and the rough places smooth. Love and justice can heal our illness and bring relief and hope for the future. The challenge is to give love and justice a chance. It is late, but humanity still has a little time to rise to its noble calling.

This book is a true story. It tells about my own personal crisis in regard to adverse actions taken against me during the course of my employment. It is the result of my painful experience and impressions derived therefrom. The experiences and tragedies of other individuals are also incorporated.

Chapters four, five, eight, nine, and ten relate some facts and names regarding this true story and my personal experience. However, the persons named in the above-referenced chapters have been changed. Any personal association with any of these names would be purely coincidental.

This book has a simple, but extraordinary message for all people. It has an urgent message for this crucial time in the history of civilization. It is mandatory reading for every person who has the responsibility of distributing values with human significance. It is mandatory reading for those who are charged with the responsibility of administering justice. Every human being who distributes and conveys values to others is a minister of justice. The distribution of human values is distributed either justly or unjustly. Almost every human trans-action has the potential for justice or injustice.

It is particularly important for those who are in superordinate positions of authority to understand the wide ramifications of the decisions affecting their subordinates. The superordinate person in authority can be a mother, father, or older sibling. The superordinate person in authority is not restricted to the President of the Country, Judges, Legislators, Governors, Mayors, Police Chiefs, Directors or Heads of Corporations and Agencies. It can be a teacher in the classroom or a referee or coach in an athletic competition. It can be anyone charged with the responsibility of distributing values equitably.

I recall an instance when my thirteen-year-old daughter worked hard in practicing along with about twelve other girls at school to become a member of a marching performance group. She was assured by the instructor that she had done well. However, the instructor, who had the authority to reduce the number of girls to a quota, did so arbitrarily. She did not just eliminate my daughter from consideration but without notice, the instructor announced the elimination of the school intercom system.

The decision and method of eliminating my daughter were devastating. It was a very violent emotional shock and psychological blow. It took considerable effort and time to heal the wound. My daughter felt that it was unfair treatment.

The perception of injustice is identified as a major mental health hazard. It can be life-threatening and fatal. Injustice is identified as a causal factor in acute mental pain, violence, and frequently, death. Persons who perceive themselves as victims of injustice frequently become fatally psychotraumatized. This psychotrauma is precipitated by the loss of something considered significantly valuable. It is not just the natural loss that causes the traumatic pain. It is the perception of an unjust loss that usually triggers the acute mental pain of psychotrauma.

The ideas in this book are an outgrowth of my personal bout with a most painful and psychotraumatic experience. I have spent ten years studying and analyzing myself and the circumstances surrounding the strange and extraordinary pain that nearly consumed my being.

As a social worker and mental health professional, I was led to study the mental and emotional crises of thousands of other persons. In addition to twelve years as a counselor and administrator in the criminal justice system, I have spent the past eight years as a clinical therapist in mental health. My specialty for the past five years has been to provide evaluations and counseling for clients in states of mental crisis. This has afforded me the opportunity to gain a more intimate knowledge and understanding of mental pain and injustice as a causal factor.

Many of the well-publicized cases involving violent deaths at the hands of longstanding, law-abiding citizens have also been analyzed and included. These cases involve persons who have lost jobs, property, human rights, and other values of significance.

In the past two years, many of the American farmers have suffered financial crises. Within these two years, a high number of farmers have committed homicide and suicide as a result of the threat to and the loss of their farms. Even as I write, The Atlanta Constitution reports that Mrs. Katherine Copeland, 55, of Chattanooga, Oklahoma, committed suicide by climbing on a pile of burning garbage on July 9, 1986. Mrs. Copeland felt that there would be a foreclosure of the family's 1,280-acre wheat and cotton farm that they had plowed since 1910. Mrs. Mona Lee Brock, who grew up with Mrs. Copeland, describes her in these words according to the Atlanta Constitution, "she was the living example of farm women - independent, staunch and upright; she was a lovely, strong lady. But in the end, the trauma of their financial problems was too much, and her strength failed her."

The information in this book is a declaration that mental injury and mental pain are real. Significant losses can and frequently are too painful to bear. The deprivations and the deficits created by these losses can precipitate an insurmountable imbalance. This is a confirmation that in its consequences, human injustice can be an intolerable stressor and a lethal one. weapon and its most remarkable effect is to cause its victims to self-destruct.

The human challenge is to overcome the insidious and destructive force of injustice, with the balancing force of love and justice. Human justice is the way to health and happiness. It is the way to survival and abundant life for all.

# CHAPTER 2

## The Psychological Essence of a Job

A job can be considered as a vessel in which one pours the substance of his life as an investment for the future. Into this vessel goes the expenditure of the most prime time, energy, and effort of one's waking hours. This vessel, called a job, requires giving, serving and contributing to the vitality of one's life. This giving is not just for a day. But it is for weeks, months and years. It demands the efforts of body, mind, emotions and sometimes, the soul. Usually, the job requires five days out of every seven and eight prime hours of each twenty-four-hour day. This vast expenditure of time and energy is an indication of just how much of a person's life is poured into a job. This substantial life expenditure is an investment for present and future returns.

A job is the primary determinant of most people's way of life. It is the major means towards a livelihood. It determines, in most instances, socioeconomic status. It means food, clothing, shelter and quality of life. Most of our activities and plans are centered around our job. Other activities are planned so that they will not conflict with our job obligations. In most of our planning, the job maintains a central place. Since a job is such a major means to significant ends, it is not uncommon for a job to take precedence over the family itself. We stay away from our family a whole work day, from eight to five for most, for the job. We often conform our behavior and suppress our political and religious ideologies for the sake of the job. Numerous and untold sacrifices are made for a job. Not only do we plan our activities around our job, but our job is frequently the primary resource that enables us to plan our other activities.

A job is a structure for a major portion of our time. It is a major vehicle for self-expression and self-actualization It provides the stage for the major role that we play in life. It provides a place and setting for our interaction with other characters. As a result of our working on a job, we develop a network of relationships with other people. Some of these relationships become primary and supportive. Some of them evolve into long-lasting, intimate, personal and social relationships. As a result of our job, we develop organizational memberships and affiliations with other agencies and institutions. The job frequently enables us to participate more fully in society as a whole. It is for many the primary doorway to the larger community and society itself. For many, it is the ladder to success and upward mobility.

A job is a major part of the individual's identity. Perhaps, more than anything else, the individual is defined by his job. When the question is asked, "Who is that person?" The typical and usual responses are as follows: "She is a schoolteacher." "He is a lawyer." "She is an accountant." "He works for a construction company." "She is a social worker." "He is a truck driver." The list goes on and on describing people by the kind of work that they do. Undoubtedly, our jobs often give us an indelible label, assign us a role, define who we are, and give us a social class rating in the hierarchy of social status. To a large degree, an individual is his profession, his job, or whatever he or she does for a living.

A job is usually thought of solely as a monetary benefit. However, the benefits of a job extend far beyond a paycheck, insurance, and retirement benefits. These benefits happen to be the most obvious and visible. As fundamental and important as they are, a job means more than a paycheck and insurance. Usually, the other intangible benefits are not recognized except in terms of a crisis that precipitated their loss. When a person is robbed of a job, somewhere during the crisis, he or she realizes that the loss is much more than money. A part of the self has been lost. Hopes and dreams have been violated.

The responsibility of recovery and vindication becomes an overwhelming duty and burden. It is a mandatory duty to put forth every effort to recover one's self, although it has been fragmented and scattered among irretrievable losses. The cry for justice is an urgent need to be whole again. It is an invocation and a petition to have one's life put back together.

What happens when the process of pouring the substance of one's life into the vessel of a job is abruptly terminated? There is a feeling that the substance of life that has been poured into the job has been lost. It is a feeling that a part of your life has been irretrievably taken away. The energy, the time and the efforts that go into a job for a period of years amount to an output as personal as one's blood.

To be cut off from the vessel where you have become accustomed to pouring your life brings about a significant impact of separation and alienation. It is not just the separation from a paycheck. It is a separation from a place, a customary routine, people, and relationships. It is a separation from a network of acquaintances and friendships. It is the separation from a major portion of one's identity. A part of whom you considered yourself to be has gone. To be cut off from the job vessel separates the terminated individual from a way of life and quality of life. It is a separation from the familiar and secure.

The traumatic separation and alienation set off a forced chain of changes and adjustments, internally and externally. The trauma of separation and alienation that create new and unfamiliar external and internal changes multiplies drastically the stress level. The terminated individual has the painful and frightening task of trying to find stability in the midst of psychological trauma and a whirlwind of changes. He also has the task of finding a new direction, new identification and a new vessel in which to pour his life.

The unjust and insensitive termination of a person from a job is one of the most destabilizing psychological traumas that a person can experience. It has far-reaching ramifications in destroying a person's psychological well-being and life.

# CHAPTER 3

## The Psychodynamics of Involuntary Job Severance

The involuntary severance from a job can be as traumatic and painful as the uninvited visit of death itself. The unexpected termination from a job can be an overwhelming psychological shock accompanied by acute and prolonged pain. The involuntary job separation frequently creates rage and a deep and profound sense of loss of something valuable and significant. It has the dual effect of inflicting severe personal injury and a feeling of deep personal loss.

In order to understand the trauma associated with being fired from a job, it is necessary to first understand what it means to lose something of significant value. When something is considered valuable to us as human beings, it has a way of becoming an intimate part of us. When we cherish something or ascribe ownership of that something of value, we tend to extend at least, a part of ourselves to that something of value.

Therefore, when something happens to the things we value and ascribe ownership, we are intimately and directly affected. The degree of the trauma associated with the loss is correlated to the object value. to the degree of significance attached to

At some point in everyone's life, a feeling associated with having lost something has been experienced. By personalizing this sense of loss, the meaning becomes clearer.

Do you recall how it felt when you lost something of value? Have you ever lost the power to carry out important commitments? Have you ever lost the ability to meet your financial obligations? Have you ever lost your pocketbook or a substantial sum of money? Have you ever lost the key to your house or to your automobile? Have you ever lost your good name or your respectable reputation? Have you ever lost a meaningful friendship or someone that you loved? Have you ever lost a future investment? Have you ever lost the fruits of your hard labor? Have you ever lost your good health, a limb, or some bodily function or ability? Have you ever lost the service of your personal resources? If you have experienced any or a combination of these losses, you probably have some sense of what it feels like to lose something of value. It is the intensity and the prolongation of this peculiar psychological pain that must be understood. If the primary causes of this peculiar pain can be understood and the isolation of the psychodynamics involved, there is the hope of preventing the pain and the frequent destructive consequences of such pain.

Involuntary job severance involves much more than just a sense of personal loss. Much more importantly, it involves a sense of personal injury. The pain from the personal injury frequently grossly supersedes the pain from the personal loss. Personal injury, not personal loss, is the primary focus of the psychotrauma involved in involuntary job severance. The substantive loss of the job can be very painful. The method of precipitating that loss can be much more painful. When a person is terminated from his job, we usually say, "He lost his job." Seldom do we say, "His job was taken."

To lose something suggests that the loss came about naturally or accidentally. Accidental and natural losses can be borne more easily than losses involving intentional deprivations. A natural loss is due to some unforeseeable circumstantial mishap. Accidental and natural losses are not accompanied by malicious thoughts or deliberate intentions to deprive or harm another person. Accidental and natural losses do not involve human conspiracies and arbitrary adverse actions against other human beings or persons who happen to be in an employment situation. It is important to make the distinction between accidental and natural losses as opposed to losses due to deliberate human engineering. The distinction is important because of the peculiar psychotrauma frequently resulting in the latter type of loss. It is important because too little attention has been given to this major cause of destructive and often violent human behavior.

To highlight and emphasize the difference and different consequences of natural losses and unnatural losses caused by human intentions, examples of both types of losses are illustrated. It is recognized that these two types of losses are construed broadly and extend beyond the work place. The examples also extend beyond the work place. However, the principles are the same and can be validly generalized.

Accidental and natural losses can be borne more easily than losses involving intentional deprivations. According to relief agencies, 1985 is on record as one of the worst years for dis- asters. These disasters have involved thousands of deaths in the African droughts, Mexican earthquake, Colombian volcanic eruption, cyclone in Bangladesh, hurricanes, tornadoes, plane crashes, and floods in the United States and other parts of the world. Thousands of accidental and natural injuries and deaths occur daily.

Accidental and natural losses produce severe pain. But be- cause the loss is natural or accidental, it is somehow easier to accept. The wounds heal more readily. The trauma is more easily overcome. Natural and accidental losses are not as psychologically threatening as losses involving deliberate and intentional deprivations.

The administrative act of terminating an employee from a job is a deliberate and intentional method of depriving an individual of a thing of value. It is not necessarily the loss of the job that triggers the traumatizing effect, rather, the method.

The method in cases of firing is an act of involuntary job severance carried out by another individual or group of individuals. The method and process of terminating a person from a job can be more painful and threatening than the actual loss of the job itself. When a person has made a considerable investment in a job, there is hardly a painless method to deprive the person of that highly valued investment. However, there are methods of job termination that range from mildly painful to acutely and critically painful. The reactions to this pain have ranged from mild depression to acute depression and outrage. This outrage has precipitated terroristic threats, aggravated as- saults, suicide and homicide.

Since the method of job termination has the potential to create acute mental pain and depression as well as violent behavior, certain questions regarding the termination of the person must be raised and considered.

The method of adverse actions in employment especially job termination has the potential for creating acute emotional and mental pain. The stressful and often excruciating pain has the potential to produce violent behavior. Violent behavior arising from arbitrary job termination has repeated itself numerous times. The human disasters resulting from these tragic consequences warrant prime attention and closer examination.

Since the brunt of the acute pain is caused by the method used in the adverse action or job termination, it would be helpful to examine the elements involved in the method. The essential question is not just what was done, but how it was done. In order to understand the trauma, some essential questions must be asked.

1.  How long has the individual been employed?
2.  How much-vested interest does the employee have in this job?
3.  What are the justifications for terminating the job?
4.  Were steps taken to avoid the necessity of terminating the employee? Was help provided to prevent the termination process?
5.  Was the employee aware that his job was in jeopardy? Was the employee informed specifically about deficiencies or complaints regarding his job?
6.  Did the employee receive fair and specific warnings regarding job deficiencies?
7.  Did the employee have an opportunity to correct the specific alleged deficiencies?
8.  Did the employee receive progressive discipline based on recognized and written professional standards?
9.  Was the employee specifically warned about the possibility of being terminated from his job?
10. Did the employee receive adequate and timely notice of his termination to present a defense before the effective date of termination?
11. Did the employee receive a fair hearing before an impartial hearing officer who has the power and authority to make an unbiased decision?

12. Was the employee fully informed of all of his employment rights?

The Courts have ruled that a job is a property right and falls under the protection of the Fourteenth Amendment of the U.S. Constitution. Failure to adequately inform, warn and give the employee an opportunity to refute allegations and accusations against him, amounts to taking the employee's job without the due process of law.

When personal property is taken without the due process of law, it is a crime of theft or robbery. When a person is terminated from his legitimate employment without the full benefit of the due process of law, a crime has been committed. A bonafide vested interest in a job is a property right. When the job is taken without the due process of law, a theft or robbery has transpired. It is a misnomer to say under such a circumstance that the person lost his job. That puts the blame on the victim of the job loss without proof. It would be more accurate to say that the job was taken or that the person was robbed of his job.

The phrase, "full benefit of the due process of law," was used to circumvent anything less than that. Many personnel offices and so-called merit systems have due process procedures, but no due process in fact. They are procedural without substance or fairness. The coverups and shams that sabotage fairness and justice add more pain and outrage. The pain is compounded by attempts to give legitimate sanction to a wrongful act. This cruel process is often designed to ignore and deny the human rights of the victimized person. The taking away of a person's job unfairly is assaulting, humiliating and dehumanizing. It is even life-threatening. Death is frequently the result.

The explanation for the acute mental pain and frequent violence associated with involuntary job severance can be found somewhere in the insensitive and unlawful method of depriving a person of employment without the due process of law.

# CHAPTER 4

## The Meaning of Job Robbery

The job robbers do more damage to their victims than street robbers. The street robber takes the money or valuables a person has in his possession at a particular time. The job robber takes away present and future earnings. When a person is fired or dismissed from his job, this is an assault upon the person, his family and his social status. Job robbery is injurious to a person's total well-being. When a person is summarily discharged from his legitimate employment, this constitutes job robbery.

### UNSUSPECTING VICTIMS

On August 20, 1975, I was fired from my government job at Metro County Family Court in Atlanta, Georgia. I had been suspended without pay five days earlier. I was a Civil Service employee with a twelve-year tenure and an impeccable record. I had invested my prime years. My wife, thirteen-year-old daughter, and I were living a fairly comfortable black middle-class family life on my $ 16,000-a-year job as a correction specialist.

With my good work record and long years of employment, I felt secure in my job. I was buying a house. I bought a new car in recent months. I was also paying for braces on my daughter's teeth. I had begun to save a few hundred dollars. I had begun to see my way out of economic deprivations. I was beginning to feel that my long years of work experience and graduate degrees were about to pay off.

I was enjoying a good community reputation. I felt that I had a lot of friends and well-wishers. After twelve years of working with children and their families, I began to see some of the fruits of my labor. Young men to whom I had given guidance in the past would come by the court to see me and express their appreciation. It was a great joy to see my old clients who also became my friends. I had many acquaintances in the criminal justice system and other social service agencies. My memberships in professional organizations were growing. I was looking forward to attending in July 1976 the twentieth-year high school reunion at Tuskegee Institute High School in Tuskegee, Alabama. My record of achievement was a modest one, but I was proud of it. I never anticipated that all these things would be shattered by job robbery.

August 1975 was the height of the worst economic depression since the early 1930s. Unemployment was at an all-time high. There were many persons with graduate degrees without work. Not only was there a job freeze but there were numerous layoffs. I was summarily terminated from my job of twelve years at such a time when jobs were almost nonexistent.

This was my first time being without a job in over twenty- three years. This called for drastic changes and a different lifestyle. My livelihood was cut off. My social status and reputation were seriously jeopardized.

What were my losses? My $16,000 yearly salary was terminated. My title of correction specialist was taken away. My membership as a peace officer in the state Peace Officers Association was terminated. My membership in the credit union was canceled. My group life and medical insurance were canceled. My automobile insurance was canceled. With the loss of my salary, I could no longer afford to pay membership dues in the other professional organizations to which I belonged. Vacation plans were canceled. Gifts and treats that I had planned for my wife and daughter were postponed. My subscriptions to professional journals and literature were canceled.

Over twelve years, my papers and effects were confiscated from my office. I acquired substantial information and research on the family court system. The robbers were not content with just taking away my job. They also stole my research material and personal effects in my office.

My contacts and associations with other agencies and community meetings were severed.

When a person is without a job his credit rating is not sufficient to borrow money. He cannot take advantage of bargains without a job. A job is the main source on which credit or financing can be secured. When a poor person's job is taken away, his right to life is taken away.

To be robbed of a job is to be robbed of friends as well. Many persons have a tendency to believe that the victim of a job robbery did something to cause his termination. Many close associates cut off their association with me.

As the months passed without having a job, my bills started getting behind. Creditors started sending their delinquent notices and referrals were made to collection agencies who harassed and threatened unmercifully. On one occasion a man from a collection agency called and attempted to threaten and intimidate me with lawsuits. He kept asking why I was not making payments. I attempted to explain to him in answer to his question that I had lost my job unfairly. He interrupted me sharply and stated, "I don't want to hear about your problems." Such unkind statements added to my despair and indignation. To be placed in a position of not being able to meet my financial obligations had the effect of exposing me and my family to insults. I felt that I had been knocked down, economically speaking, and those who got the least opportunity attempted to trample me. This was especially true of creditors and collection agencies. These insults were made possible because I had been robbed of my job.

To be without a job is to be without the means to provide and protect one's family. A source of income is necessary for a productive life in our modern society. I became more keenly aware of the many things I wanted to do for my family when I did not have an income. It was a damaging blow to my pride and self-esteem to be without an income to support my family. Excuses are not sufficient substitutes for providing support and services for one's family. Despite these reasons, life does not kindly excuse a man for being without a job and without an income to support his family. I got the feeling from many acquaintances that they were not convinced that I did not contribute to my job termination. There is a strong tendency to blame the victims. I also got the impression that they were not concerned about my predicament of having been illegally deprived of a job. There was no rush to provide any kind of support. Those who promised support did not follow through in 99 percent of the cases. My experience taught me that there is a frightening shortage of, "Good Samaritans" who travel the roads of the wounded and robbed.

## IMPOSED HANDICAPS OF JOB ROBBERY

In addition to the financial crisis and reduced social status resulting from my job robbery, a host of other handicaps were imposed on me. The illegal action of depriving me of my job and my subsequent losses and pain were just a small part of the meaning of job robbery. Job robbery is accomplished through administrative lies and judicial deceptions. It is not only designed to take away the victim's present livelihood but to minimize his living opportunities for the future as well. It is designed to prevent a person from providing, protecting, and producing for himself and his family. An economic right is one of the most basic of human rights. Job robbery violates a person's present economic rights. It deprives him of an equal employment opportunity by imposing a serious personal and social handicap.

The major imposed handicaps that I suffered as a result of my job being taken away were the following: (1) My financial resources and my opportunities for acquiring financial resources were significantly reduced. (2) The persisting stigma of being fired from a job damaged my reputation and my chances for other gainful employment. (3) I was compelled to pursue the nonpaying job of looking for a job. (4) It was necessary that I function on a high level in the midst of family pain and personal crisis. (5) It became my responsibility to struggle for justice against unrightable wrongs. Those imposed handicaps combined as a weight and a burden that were too heavy and too painful to be borne by any individual. A further exploration of these handicaps will help to understand the damaging effects of the abominable crime of job robbery.

## (1) LIMITED RESOURCES AND OPPORTUNITIES

When my salary was terminated on August 15, 1975, for the first time in twenty-three years I was without an income. My financial liabilities immediately exceeded my assets. The home of which I was buying was jeopardized. The automobile that I had bought less than a year was jeopardized. Other bills that I had must be paid each month. However, without an income, my financial obligations could not be met. It was not just the termination of my income that concerned me, but everything else that we had accumulated was jeopardized. The loss of an income causes the immediate corrosion of all other assets. Being poor, those assets were very limited. As with most poor people we lived primarily from paycheck to paycheck.

The black and the poor cannot have economic security when they do not have job security. If a civil service employee of twelve years with an impeccable work record can have his job taken without reason, there is no job security. Therefore, there is no economic security for a black or a poor person. A job is all that they have.

Job robbery comes as a thief in the night, under cover of darkness and without warning. Therefore, there is no time to prepare for such a crime. Since the black and the poor are al- ways more vulnerable, there is no way for them to prevent the crime of job robbery. When it happens, their already scarce economic resources are soon depleted.

The same illegal action that robbed me of my job deprived me of the necessary financial resources to defend myself of the crime committed against me. I was placed at a severe dis- advantage to defend myself at the very time the violation took place. At the time I needed more money to defend myself, I had less. Job robbery has the dual effect of violating its victim's rights and depriving him of an adequate opportunity to defend himself. The handicap of being without a job is the handicap of being without a defense. I was robbed of my financial resources and consequently deprived of the opportunity or means to acquire financial resources.

The man who committed job robbery against me is continuing to be paid out of taxpayer's money. The Civil Service Board defending his actions is paid out of taxpayer's money. The attorneys representing the man who robbed me of my job are paid by the Metro County taxpayers. The man who violated the law mandated by the U.S. Constitution after twelve years has not been brought to justice. Criminals are still at large. Criminals are still on the taxpayer's payroll. To add insult to injury, I as a U.S. citizen, resident, voter and taxpayer of Metro County, am also helping to pay the salary of the man who robbed me of my job.

## (2) THE PERSISTING STIGMA OF BEING FIRED FROM A JOB

To get fired from a job is damaging to a person's reputation no matter how innocent he is of any wrong doing. Certain persons who have been close acquaintances will avoid associating with a person who has been fired from a job. The stigma persists and continues to do damage. It closes many doors of opportunity.

An explanation as to why people generally get fired from their jobs will help to understand the persisting stigma of job robbery. Keep in mind that the reasons given for firing a per- son from his job may or may not be true. Generally, the rea- sons given for terminating a person's employment are alleged insubordination, incompetence, violation of law or policy or some behavior involving moral turpitude. All of these things conjure up ugly images in the minds of people. Job prospects for persons who are guilty or persons who are accused of any of the above allegations are significantly reduced.

What employer is willing to hire someone who has been fired for challenging or threatening his previous employer? How many employers are willing to risk hiring someone who has been dismissed from previous employment for unsatisfactory job performance? Who is willing to hire someone who has apparently demonstrated a lack of respect for the company or agency policies? Most legitimate employers would frown on the idea of hiring someone whose moral behavior or integrity was questionable. Frequently, Black job applicants who were fired from a previous job for insubordination to a White person are perceived as a Black militant or an uppity Negro. Too often, there is an automatic assumption that the victim of job robbery is guilty. Even when not expressed it is felt by many that the victim is to blame for his job termination. The general feeling is that "He must have done something wrong to get fired."

The stigma of being fired from a job makes a person more vulnerable to discriminatory hiring practices. The Merit System of Georgia provides a ground for rejecting a qualified job applicant on the basis the applicant was fired from his previous job. No further explanation is needed for rejecting a qualified job applicant. In most instances, the applicant who has been fired from a previous job is at the mercy of the prospective employer, even for the Civil Service jobs.

The merit system job applications are often designed to in- criminate, interrogate, and even intimidate the applicant who has been fired from a previous job. In addition to several pages of personal questions, they specifically ask, were you ever fired from a government job. Any false statements can be grounds to reject applications or dismiss the applicant after he is hired. A person who has been fired from a job is faced with double jeopardy when he applies for another job with the State Merit System. He is compelled to incriminate himself. If he reveals that he was fired from a government job, he risks not getting the job. If he lies he risks being fired for false statements after he gets the job. Is it fair for a person who has been fired from a job to be deprived of an equal opportunity for another job? Has a person who has been fired from a job lost his civil rights?

The present application for the State of Georgia employment requires that a person incriminate himself by stating on the application that he has been fired from a previous job. That question is used along with other questions, such as, have you ever been convicted of a felony?

The right to an equal employment opportunity under the present system and laws is insecure and fragile. It is not guaranteed. It is not protected. The law is not enforced. If so, it is done on a very limited and selective basis. It takes only one biased individual in a hiring position to prevent the fulfillment of the right of equal employment opportunity. He can deny the right to a job and not be held accountable for his arbitrary actions.

The state of affairs in this regard is that an individual who is paid out of public funds exercises the power to deny a U.S. citizen, tax-paying resident, and voter a Civil Service job at his discretion. There is absolutely no assurance that the best-qualified applicant will get the job. The loopholes in the qualifying, screening, and selection process are so numerous that the so-called Merit System becomes a misnomer. It is a non-merit system.

## (3) THE JOB OF LOOKING FOR A JOB

The most unfulfilling job is the job of looking for a job. This is the most visible handicap imposed by job robbery. It requires that the victim start all over again exposing himself and subjecting himself to repeated arrogance, humiliation, and rejections. He must suspend his pride and hide his anger. The search for a job becomes all-consuming for his time, energy, and dwindling resources. This apprehensive and sacrificial job search provides no guarantees and no pay.

When it became evident that the wheels of justice would not turn in my favor and that I would not be reinstated to my job, I began seeking other employment. Since I had been working as a classified government employee for twelve years, I sought employment with the Federal, State, and Local governments. Although I had learned from bitter experiences that the Merit System offered no job protection, I wanted another Merit System job. I wanted to learn about merit systems and further test my rights as a citizen and government employee. I was in for a lot more education about the state Merit System. This will be explored in more detail later.

Along about the same time I started looking for a job in the fall of 1975, I also applied for unemployment compensation at the Georgia Labor Department on Marietta Street in Atlanta. The unemployment lines were very long. I spent two days registering and applying. One of the first questions was why I left my last job. The question was raised as to whether a person who was fired from his job would be eligible for unemployment compensation. Another question was whether a person who was fired from his previous job would get the full amount. Each time I had an interview I found my- self on the defensive. It was necessary for me to go through the pain of talking about the ordeal of my job robbery over and over.

The long lines of unemployed people seeking survival compensation were a demeaning scene of debased humanity. It was a depressing scene of wasted time and wasted lives. It was a scene that devalued and cheapened human life. It reduces the feelings of self-worth and self-esteem. It is one of the many dumping grounds for the putdown and rejection in society. I am a part of this junk pile of humanity. I felt embarrassed, alienated, angry, and dehumanized.

The procedure and red tape required to apply and get un- employment compensation damage personal pride and destroy respect for the government. The demeaning long lines and frustrating red tape seem to be a part of the lives of the economically deprived. A great portion of their lives is spent in long lines, crowded waiting rooms, and going through red tape interrogation. The vast majority of these people are the Blacks and the poor whites. Since there are no safe and secure jobs for the Blacks and the poor, most of us could find our- selves in the long lines of red tape interrogation.

While standing in the long lines and the crowded waiting rooms I had the occasion to talk with some of the applicants for unemployment compensation. The dominant thoughts that run through their minds were that "Nobody gives a damn." "The system is unfair." They felt that those who cared could not help and those who could help did not care. I have not seen convincing evidence to suggest that they are wrong.

I received several months of unemployment compensation in the latter part of 1975 and the beginning of the year 1976. During this time, I was subjected to hours of long lines and long waits each week. The check was cut off several times without explanation. This required going to the

Labor Department and waiting for hours to ask why the check was cut off. I was not able to get any information by telephone. The Labor Department personnel required personal appearance for insignificant details. Unemployment compensation is not issued without great cost to the applicant's self-esteem and personal pride.

Job hunting is expensive and time-consuming. To compete effectively for the scarce jobs, I carefully prepared a resume and had numerous copies made. I mailed many and took others to prospective employers. I filled out numerous applications for Federal, State, County, and City jobs. Many days and nights were spent filling out job applications. Many miles were traveled, and many hours were spent on job interviews. Most were unproductive. All of these jobs applied for were through Merit Systems. If there was a fair selection process, it did not seem so to me as an applicant.

Over and over, I was faced with employees on the government payrolls who played games and politics with government jobs. They wasted my time at interviews. In many instances, I was well qualified for the job and did not get any reasons for not being selected for the job.

I was interviewed for a Volunteer Coordinator Job at Georgia Mental Health Hospital in January 1976. I received a favorable impression from the person who had previously held the job. I was interviewed by a committee of four persons several days later. The impression was favorable. I was seen by the Director of the GMHH, and he stated that my termination from my other job was bad for me and bad for them. He used that as a reason for rejecting me. This was done after filling out an application and returning for several interviews.

I was later turned down for a Social Worker position by one person at GMHH. He looked at my resume and stated that I did not have enough medical training because the position required prescribing and administering medicine. I did not argue with him because I was not licensed to practice medicine.

There was a vacancy for a Planner with a CJS (Criminal Justice System) background in the State OMB section. I was sent by a helpful Merit System counselor. After several interviews, I was placed on an indefinite waiting list, although the vacancy was there and definite.

As the rejections continued I began to lose confidence in our Merit System. It was not a Merit System. Each rejection was an added blow, a worse letdown.

The job of looking for a job or the process of trying to get a job for me was a vicious process. It was an unfair process. I was subjected to this process because I had been robbed of my previous job. Those who robbed me of my job and those who rejected me for another job were working jointly, prevent- ing me from employment. In the non-merit system, all things work together for bad.

The time and energy consumed by looking for a job leave very little time and energy for other tasks. My whole life suffered. The procession of life for me came to a standstill. A system that allows the robbery of a job and a conspiracy to keep a head of household from getting a job is cruel and extraordinary punishment. It is a crime against humanity.

## (4) FAMILY PAIN AND PERSONAL CRISIS

My personal life and family life were shrouded in a cloud of darkness and despair. It was as if someone was blocking the light of the sun by day and the moon by night. It seemed that the clean fresh air had been polluted with bitterness and poison. It was most difficult to see through this dark cloud of despair and through this atmosphere of bitterness and poison. It was an atmosphere of tension, anxiety, apprehension, fatigue, irritation, indignation, depression, and hurt. The experience was much worse than being surrounded by a dark cloud. It was like being engulfed by a net of wickedness and a veil of evil.

For weeks and weeks, this cloud hovered over my life and my family. At numerous points, I was tempted to give up. It required a force beyond my strength to keep me going. I felt so ill at times that had I given up for one second I would have lost my health and probably my life. I felt all the symptoms of a physically sick person. It meant that I must not go to bed. It meant that I must keep going. It meant that I must not seek relief from chemicals or doctors. Chemically induced sedation or elation was not an answer to my problems.

I developed a tendency to withdraw from social relationships. More and more I was isolating myself. My interest in outside activities was curtailed. I did not have the enthusiasm to reach out to others. I usually attended church every Sun- day and other church activities at least once during the week. My church attendance was reduced to once or twice per month. I found myself placing significant limitations on contacts outside of my immediate family.

This was not just a withdrawal from social activities. I am also inclined to withdraw within myself and my own home. I lost interest in doing certain chores around the house. There was a compelling force reverting my interests and my thoughts inwardly.

It seemed as if the procession of life for me came to a standstill. I had been forced to the sideline of life. I could hear life and see life passing by without me. I was reminded of my own insignificance. Because the stream of life rushes on in spite of those who drop out or are forced out. It does not stop or tarry. It does not weep or embrace. It goes its merry way. Like Old Man River, it keeps rolling along.

Being outside of that stream of life is a lonely and alienated existence. My separation and alienation from this stream of life were painful. This pain was concentrated primarily in my personal life and family life. However, I could not abdicate my- self from the responsibility of a husband, father, and adult. I still had obligations to meet as a citizen. There are no exemptions from these responsibilities. Even if you are forced out of the stream of life or if you drop out on your own, life does not excuse you.

Along with the pain, there is still the responsibility and accountability for your life. I found it much more difficult to meet my responsibilities with all the pain in my life and my family. This was a most serious handicap imposed by my being robbed of a job. With my personal crisis and family pain, I was still expected to fulfill all obligations. I still must produce, protect, and provide for my family and for myself.

What effect does it have on a man to face his family week after week without a job? Although I had a good excuse for being without a job after having been robbed of the same, after a while the excuse wears thin. Good excuses for being without a job do not support a family. They do not buy food or provide shelter.

Sympathetic feelings toward the victim of job robbery do not last indefinitely. These feelings can very shortly turn to contempt. The world does not allow indefinite time to weep. Job robbery effects are not necessarily temporary. The effects get worse as time goes on. As time passes and the pain worsens, the sympathy and support of others grow weaker. As time passed, the distance and relationships between acquaintances could not be found. The security of my wife and family was seriously undercut. My thirteen-year-old daughter became more and more anxious about my not having a job. It was difficult to give assurances while laboring under such severe handicaps. How could I give assurance to my thirteen-year-old child when unchecked injustices had robbed me of my own assurance?

The atmosphere of my family life wreaked with pain. The hurt we felt in our hearts radiated through our whole being. It was living on the verge of tears and at the edge of despair. I wanted to scream for relief. But I could not afford to scream, It would be like pushing the panic button of a mental breakdown of my family. I knew that they felt like screaming too, but refrained because they also wanted to act brave as we wandered through a tunnel of darkness and hurt. We carried on as best we could the functions of family living. But underneath our activities, and our attempts to be brave and strong, there was an undercurrent of severe pain. Panic and terror were threatening to overwhelm us at any time.

## (5) THE STRUGGLE FOR JUSTICE

Job robbery imposes on its victim the job of struggling for justice. This is a serious handicap because I was placed in a disadvantageous position of having to put forth extra effort and resources to obtain something that already belonged to me. When a person becomes a victim and a witness of a job robbery, it becomes his responsibility to correct the wrongs.

Struggling for justice for me became synonymous with struggling to protect my reputation, to make a living, to correct my record, to maintain my health, and to overcome the hurt and damage to me and my family. It became synonymous with living.

I do not seek vengeance, but I do seek vindication. Why should the victim of injustice take on the awesome and seemingly impossible task of correcting an unrightable wrong against overwhelming odds? The pursuit of justice for a mistreated victim becomes as vital for his life as oxygen is for suffocating lungs. The pursuit of justice becomes a necessary ingredient for survival. Anyone who has been severely damaged by injustice realizes the importance of placing justice as a top priority on his agenda. The price of justice is high. The price of injustice is higher. The struggle for justice is less costly than the voluntary acquiescence to injustice. To sit and do nothing does not diminish mental pain. It might even prolong mental suffering. More importantly, inaction on the part of the victim takes away from his own soul.

The goal of a just society is consistent with the goals of religion and democracy at their highest peak. It is consistent with the kingdom of God, with life and salvation. No matter what the sacrifice may be, I must climb out of this dark pit of injustice. I must climb over this mountain of evil deeds and reach the end of this tunnel of unrighteousness. My life depends on and my soul longs for the fresh air of justice and the beauty of peace.

I felt that I must fight against my victimization with every resource available. The reason the overwhelming odds did not deter me was that I had that feeling that I had everything to gain and everything to lose.

Job robbery means to take away by unjust means, a person's right to earn a living. It means to deprive him of economic means to survive. It is designed to stop the victim's social progress and personal development.

Job robbery is an attempt to destroy a person by taking away his legitimate means of earning a living. Job robbery clouds the life of its victim with helplessness, hopelessness and pain. Job robbery means to suffer simultaneously a multiplicity of social handicaps and personal crises.

Job robbery is a merciless assault upon the victim and his family. It means family deprivation and family pain. It destroys hopes and dreams. Job robbery disavows justice and equality under the law. It makes a lie of democracy. It ignores professional ethics and religious values. It is a roughshod trampling over human feelings and human rights. Job robbery presents a physical and mental health hazard. It is a threat to one's life and the total well-being of his family. The magnitude of such a crime must be responded to by a continuous struggle for justice.

When a person is unlawfully terminated from his job he loses much more than just a job. Not only is his property interest affected because of a legally recognized vested interest, but also a liberty interest is adversely affected. It was not just the termination of an income that was so injurious and damaging to me. My reputation and status in the community were also affected. My professional status and the domestic tranquility of my home were severely disrupted. The adverse actions set off a chain reaction that compounded my damage and pain.

# CHAPTER 5

## How Injustice Causes Pain, Violence and Death

Injustice can be and often is a lethal stressor. It has damaging effects on the body, mind and spirit. It can cause irreparable damage to one's physical and mental health. It can obliterate future hope. It can cause acute and intolerable pain and severe injuries within. It can cause violence and death without. The outward violence and homicidal consequences have a direct relationship to a unique internal condition precipitated by a perception of injustice. The news media are replete with the external violent consequences of persons who have perceived themselves as victims of injustice. The external consequences are obvious. The primary focus of this work will be on the internal effects of injustice. The objective is to provide some insight into the mental, emotional and spiritual crisis within.

### THE NATURE OF INJUSTICE

Injustice is an unwarranted adverse action against another person. It is disparate treatment. It comes in many forms. It is manifested in many ways. It may be an unkind word, an arrogant attitude, a cold indifference or a disrespectful gesture. It can be unfairness and unkindness. Injustice may be in the form of discriminatory rejection and subordination. It may be an intimidating frown or threatening words. It can manifest itself in the misrepresentation of truth. It may be in the form of benign neglect, evil silence or criminal negligence. It is an unrighteous act that takes unfair advantage. It is a means of exploitation through dishonesty and deception. Injustice is a violation of human rights. The primary human rights have been enumerated as being the right to life, liberty, ownership of property and the pursuit of happiness. A human right is a God-given right. It is a right to know the truth. It is a right to develop the human potential to the optimum. It is a right to self-actualization and self-determination. It is a right to an abundant life.

Injustice reduces and robs life. It steals liberty and confiscates ownership. It sabotages happiness. Injustice is a denial of human rights. It enslaves life and oppresses freedom. It puts dark clouds in a sunny sky and transforms our days into darkness. Injustice turns pleasant dreams into frightening nightmares.

Injustice is a thief, a rapist, a robber and a murderer. It is a terroristic weapon in the hands of a criminal. It's a lie that defames goodness. It's a spear that pierces innocence. It's a sword that cuts righteousness. It's a gun that shoots at the truth. It's a bomb that explodes in the midst of peace. It's a poison that defiles cleanliness. It corrupts purity and spoils beauty.

Injustice is an infectious spiritual disease. It is a malignancy that cannot be observed under a microscope or isolated in a test tube. It cannot be harnessed for study in our scientific laboratories. But it is as damaging as high blood pressure or diabetes. It is as deadly as cancer, suicide or homicide. It is as real as a man going berserk and killing his supervisor. It is as real as the apartheid system in South Africa. It is a disease that often causes a major disharmony and malfunction of the human organism. It is often the root of social unrest and political revolutions. This disease is invisible to the naked eye. It has no known physical existence. But its poisonous and lethal effects manifest themselves most dramatically, in physical and mental illness, as well as antisocial and violent behavior. Injustice is invisible and elusive. But it has a morbid existence somewhere in the matrix of human relationships and the human decision-making process.

There is no known immunity from the effects or attack of injustice. All human beings are vulnerable. To highlight the spiritual nature of this disease, the Apostle Paul reminded the Ephesians, "Tor we wrestle not against flesh and blood, but against principalities, against powers, against the rulers of the darkness of this world, against spiritual wickedness in high places."

Injustice is not new. It is as old as the human race. What is new is an examination of the unique psychological effects of injustice upon its victims. It is a close-up look at the acute psychotrauma that frequently accompanies injustice victimization. Throughout history, the acts of injustice are well documented. However, the psychotrauma associated with injustice (not the acts of injustice) has not received sufficient attention. Injustice is a major stressor that needs recognition and consideration.

## THE STRESS CRISIS OF INJUSTICE

A stressor produces mental, emotional and physical tension. The muscles tighten and contract. Feelings are painfully compressed and pressured. The mind becomes painfully obsessed and preoccupied. As the stressor or stressors increase the tension, the rigidity and uneasiness of the body increase. This rigidity and uneasiness can reach intolerable limits. This condition is called a stress crisis. It is frequently produced by what is perceived as injustice.

A stressor is anything that threatens one's life or well-being or the life and well-being of those you love. In milder forms, a stressor may be anything that creates anxiety or disturbs a state of restfulness or tranquility.

Life is filled with stressors. Stress is not necessarily good or bad. Stress serves as a motivator for one to overcome anxiety and discomfort. It prepares and conditions one to solve problems, circumvent and if necessary, to meet danger. It can be an incentive to plan for future security. Stress elicits a variety of responses. In an effort to regain equilibrium and stability after a stressful disturbance, the response to the stress is most crucial.

Different stressors elicit and stimulate different responses. Responses may be physical, mental, emotional, chemical or combinations of the four responses. The physical, mental and emotional responses are more commonly recognized and analyzed.

However, in this presentation, it is the chemical responses that will be addressed in addition to the others. It is hypothesized that the chemical responses in the human organism are a primary influence upon the mental, emotional and physical responses. This is especially suspected to be true during the stress crisis precipitated by injustice. During a stress crisis, certain chemical transformations take place within the body. Certain chemicals, in disproportions, are injected into the bloodstream by the endocrine glands. These chemical substances, called hormones, could be the key factor in understanding the pain, violence and death caused by injustice.

The physical responses to injustice (or perceptions of injustice) are more apparent because of their openness and visibility. However, precedent to the physical responses, mental and emotional responses have already taken place. A physical response is also meant to include legal and behavioral responses. Many of the behavioral responses indicate most dramatically, the tragic seriousness of the problem of injustice and the acute psychotrauma it causes. The extremely violent reactions to the perception of injustice and victimization provide convincing testimony and irrefutable evidence that injustice is often a lethal stressor.

The news media are replete with violent behavior in response to unfair or unjust treatment. Since many of these incidents are not highly publicized, we are probably witnessing the "tip of the iceberg," situation.

The following well-publicized cases are presented to illustrate the violent reactions of persons who have been traumatized by injustice or the perception of injustice. These violent reactions are often directed towards self as well as others. These cases illustrate fatal violent reactions resulting from the lethal stress of injustice.

On November 27, 1978, Dan White, a thirty-two-year-old white man and former supervisor with the city of San Francisco, California, shot to death Mayor George Mo- scone with his service revolver. He then went down the hall and fatally wounded Harvey Milk, the first avowed homosexual to be elected to the City's Board of Supervisors.

Prior to the shooting, Dan White had gone to Mayor Moscone's office to ask the Mayor for his job back that he had resigned from seventeen days earlier. White stated to the Mayor that he and his family could not live on the $9,600 salary. Mayor Moscone refused to give White's job back and that triggered the shooting deaths of Mo- scone and Milk.

White was convicted of voluntary manslaughter instead of murder, after his lawyer, Douglas Schmidt, argued that White suffered from, "diminished capacity." (Dan White was released from prison in 1984. He committed suicide on October 21, 1985.)

Dan White, the former police officer and firefighter had a very good reputation before the tragedy that occurred on November 27, 1978. He was said to be a law-abiding and religious man. He was said to be a hardworking, honest family man. He did not smoke, drink or use drugs. He had a reputation for being a responsible and conscientious public servant.

[The source of information gathered on Dan White was taken from the Atlanta Constitution Newspaper and a television documentary on November 27, 1984.]

What were the psychodynamics that caused the rapid and dramatic transformation in Dan White from a peaceful law-abiding citizen to an outraged man who shoots two people to death?

On Wednesday, March 6, 1985, as reported by the Atlanta Constitution, a postal worker, Stephen W. Brown- lee, pulled a handgun from his pants pocket gunned down his supervisor and a co-worker, and wounded a third man. This incident took place at the main post office in Atlanta, Georgia.

Brownlee had worked at the post office for twelve years. He was married and the father of two children. Brownlee, a black man, feared he was the target of whites who were going to get him because he was black. He harbored perceptions of racial injustice in regard to his employment.

What is it that makes a responsible government employee of twelve years, a family man, the father of two children, suddenly become a multiple killer?

The Atlanta Constitution (March 17, 1985) reported that on March 16, 1985, in Connellsville, Pennsylvania, Mansel "Sonny" Hammett, a factory worker who had just been suspended from his job, pistol whipped his way into the plant and killed four foremen and critically wounded a fifth, then shot himself to death.

Hammett, 39, had been suspended for disciplinary reasons. He was a father of two sons and had worked at the plant since he graduated from high school. He was from Dumbar, Pennsylvania. Co-workers said, "He just went berserk." His priest said that he had been in church the last night.

What is the nature of the rage that would provoke an ordinary peaceful and responsible man to go berserk and kill four people?

On February 19, 1986, as reported by the Atlanta Constitution, Ed Hernandez, 24, of New York City, armed with a shotgun, took two people hostage at the H & R Block tax office where he had been fired the day before. He freed them after a four-hour standoff. He remained inside the building, threatening suicide. He held hostage, the office manager, Phyllus Novick and her son, Michael. As reported by the Constitution, Hernandez's parole officer, mother and a police chaplain were brought in by helicopter to speak with him.

There appears to be something extraordinary that is associated with being fired from a job that creates severe rage and provokes violent actions. An analysis of the extraordinary ingredient is the subject of this work.

The Atlanta Constitution reported three cases of violent behavior associated with the financial crisis of some American farmers. While it is true that these farmers were not fired from their jobs, the consequence of having benefits terminated illustrates an overwhelming force that precipitates violent behavior in men who are not considered violent by any stretch of the imagination:

On December 9, 1985, sixty-three-year-old Dale Burr, a farmer of Hills, Iowa, whose financial troubles were about to claim his land, his machinery, his stored grain and his beloved horses, went on a killing rampage, shooting three people to death before committing suicide himself. He shot Emily, his wife of forty years. He left a note at home and drove into town. He shot the bank president where he had an overdrawn checking account. He drove east of town a few miles and was seen shooting once into the air. At 11:35 a.m., Burr entered the farm yard of Richard Goody, with whom he had had a minor land dispute several years ago. As the thirty-six-year-old Goody greeted him, Burr shot him twice. He also fired at Goody's fleeing wife and six-year-old son. Ten minutes later when he was pulled over by a sheriff's deputy, a muffled blast from within the pickup indicated he had shot himself. He had debts upward of over $800,000 that were past due the last Friday.

What is the explanation of this rampage of killing by a sixty-three-year-old family man who had lived a successful and productive life?

On January 8, 1986, Bruce Litchfield, 38, of Elk Point, South Dakota, a farm loan supervisor, shot his wife and two children to death in their sleep, then went to his office and turned the gun on himself. His efforts to help farmers in financial trouble failed. He left a note, "The job got pressure on my mind, pain on the left side."

What was the nature of this "pressure" and "pain" that would cause a man to shoot his wife and two children and then kill himself? What happened to his brain, his reasoning and his judgment?

The third farm financial crisis case was related by the Atlanta Constitution as follows:

For a solid decade, Leonard Dozier Hill, III, age sixty-seven of Waynesborough, Georgia, lived on hope. He hoped for a turnabout in the weather and the lagging profits on farm commodities to save the 1300 acres that had been in his family for four generations. Hill's hopes ran out on Tuesday, February 4, 1986. Seven hundred eleven acres of his farm where he had raised cotton, wheat, corn and soybeans, were to be auctioned off from the steps of the Burke County Courthouse to satisfy a $62,000 note held by the

Federal Land Bank of Central Georgia and the Farmers Production Credit Association. The auction was scheduled for 11:00 a.m. About 10:40 a.m. he shot and killed himself with a 22-caliber rifle. He left a wife of forty-six years, two sons, three daughters and eleven grandchildren.

What happens to the central nervous system and the mind when hope runs out? What are the effects of the perception of a hopeless existence upon a person's life? What causes a person to choose death rather than to live without hope?

On January 31, 1986, the Atlanta Constitution reported that in Newport, Rhode Island:

A Black Navy sailor was found guilty in January 1986, of premeditated murder in the fatal stabbing of a white lieutenant at sea. Petty Officer Mitchell T. Garroway, Jr. allegedly killed Lieutenant James K. Sterner on June 16, 1985, aboard the USS Miller. Civilian defense attorney Lawyer Trevor L. Brooks said the murder was committed in a spontaneous fit of rage. Garroway had also perceived racism and unfair treatment in relation to a job promotion.

The Black sailor testified in court that he was a target of racism and he "just snapped" when he killed his white superior officer, Lieutenant James Sterner, 35, of Woodbridge, New Jersey.

We often hear of people "going berserk" or "just snapped", when some violent act has been committed. What do the expressions of "going berserk" or "just snapped" mean?

What can be done to prevent people from snapping and going berserk?

The news is replete with men going berserk and killing people, usually in a fit of rage in regards to some painful perception of unfair or degrading treatment.

*Tjq dMai aäjr d* September 23, 1985, issue, gives the following account of a bludgeoning death:

On August 1978, Theodore Streleski, 42, grabbed a sledgehammer, confronted his math professor, Karl de Leevw at Standford University and viciously bludgeoned him to death. Streleski had languished at Standford University for nineteen years trying to complete his dissertation for his doctorate in mathematics. His frustrations boiled over and resulted in his murdering Professor de Leevw. Streleski felt that Stanford treated students "Criminally". He served seven years in a California Prison. Upon his release on September 8, 1985, he gave no assurance that he would not kill again under similar circumstances. He offered no apology for the murder of Professor de Leevw.

Again, the question is raised, how awful and acute must be the pain that would provoke such vengeful violence? The magnitude of pain that would provoke such an extreme act of violence must have a connotation that is not well-known or understood by the general public. What was so awful and outrageous in the experience of Theodore Streleski, that after seven years of prison, he felt justified in bludgeoning to death his mathematics professor?

On Thursday, April 3, 1986, John Pasch, Jr. of Chicago, killed his landlord and a police officer and held an elderly woman hostage for thirty-five hours. On Sunday, April 6, 1986, the Atlanta Constitution gives the following account:

Chicago - A heavily armed man who held an elderly woman hostage after killing his landlord and a police officer surrendered peacefully Saturday, ending a marathon standoff that police had vowed to end without bloodshed.

Pasch, who weighed 300 pounds and was described by neighbors and friends as a "pretty lonely" man who lost his job as a machinist six years ago, was charged with two counts of murder at a morning hearing and jailed without bond.

After entering the building where Pasch had held neighbor Jean Wiwatowski captive, police found a revolver with 300 rounds of ammunition and a rifle with 150 rounds of ammunition "stacked up and ready to go," said police Commander Edward Wadnicki.

The standoff began about 3 p.m. Thursday when Pasch, who was months behind on his rent, shot and killed his landlord, Leslie Shearer, 45, who had come to talk to him about it, said police superintendent Fred Rice.

Officer Richard Clark, a member of the department's tactical unit, was shot to death by Pasch as he responded to reports of gunfire, Rice said. Clark, 48, a decorated eighteen-year veteran of this force, was not in uniform at the time.

The individuals in the preceding case studies suffered acute psychological trauma resulting from their job loss and threat to their livelihood. The traumatic losses created more pain than they could tolerate without an emotional explosion. Their violent behavior was in response to their perception of an injustice perpetrated against them. The stimulus of injustice elicited an extreme response of violence. The acts of violence in each case represented a compelling need to release the unbearable painful tension and stress.

In each case, there was a significant loss or deprivation. The losses involved an income or the loss of resources to produce income. In each case, the traumatized individuals had invested a substantial amount of time and effort in their respective endeavors. In each case, there was an expression of desperation arising out of a feeling of helplessness and hopelessness. In each case, the traumatized person acted alone without any apparent consultation with anyone else. The violent acts represented the epitome of personal vengeance and vindication.

These men who committed violent murder and suicide were not psychopathic killers or antisocial personalities. They did not kill for pleasure. They did not kill for money or material gain. They killed and committed violence to relieve their unbearable pain and their outrageous indignation. Their violence was directed toward persons thought to be responsible for their pain. In some instances, their violence was directed toward themselves when their pain reached unbearable limits. In some instances, their violence was directed toward family members in an attempt to safeguard family members from the acute pain that they had already experienced. The pain was so intense that they felt it was an act of mercy to kill family members to spare them from the agonizing pain.

The unfair, unexpected and arbitrary termination from a job or livelihood often produces lethal stress and violent reactions. It causes good law-abiding citizens to become violent murderers. Healthy and successful men have suddenly withdrawn into suicidal depression because of adverse actions in their employment. Good family providers and churchgoing men have been transformed into rampaging killers. We have witnessed men with good reputations, hardworking and constructive living, suddenly, erupt into violent killers.

The primary reasons for the murders and violence in each case presented were to relieve and prevent further unbearable pain. Violent retribution towards those who are perceived as having committed the injustice serves to relieve the pain and vindicate the injustice.

The fact that these men chose violence, indicates that they had either exhausted other options, unaware of them or had no faith in other options. Out of their helplessness, hopelessness- ness and pain they were compelled by a psychotraumatic crisis in the mind to take the most extreme actions to put an end to a nightmare. They took drastic and violent actions to end a nightmare that haunts, stalks and frightens not just during the night and during sleep, but during the night and day and during every awakened hour.

# CHAPTER 6

## Violent Human Behavior is Preventable

There is an answer to the cause of violent human behavior. In most instances, the cause of violent human behavior is no mystery. In most cases, it has a direct connection to an event or a definite set of circumstances. The event or set of circumstances can be identified and isolated. Usually, the precipitating event or circumstances, once isolated, are easy to analyze.

The circumstances that precipitate violent behavior can often be identified, understood and predicted. Therefore, it is not difficult to establish the rationale behind violent human behavior. It is amazing that so much is generally known about the causes of violent behavior but so little is specifically done to prevent it.

There is an urgent need for political leaders, judicial decision makers, professionals, agencies and all persons who deal with individuals predisposed to become violent, to understand the primary reasons behind that type of behavior. It is suspected that many people feel that if they attempt to under- stand or acknowledge the causes of violence, it may be interpreted as condoning the violence.

However, to acknowledge the cause or understand the reasons for violence is not synonymous to a justification of that violence. The threatening and destructive nature of violence creates such an intolerance that the usual response is to attempt to suppress it or to overpower it with more violence. These typical responses continue to perpetuate the attitude of overlooking the precipitating causes of violence. The popular tendency to overlook the causes is a primary barrier to violence prevention. Specific acts precipitate a predisposition toward violent behavior. There is overwhelming evidence that supports the contention that violent behavior is a response to pain or to the threat of pain. The specific acts that produce pain or the threat of pain can happen instantly, or they can accumulate over a period of time. One threatening act or an act that is perceived to be threatening can produce a violent response in the person perceiving the threat. On the other hand, a series of acts over a period of time can accumulate and produce a violent response.

Many of the causes of violence are covert, hidden and clandestine. They operate underneath the surface. They frequently operate in disparaging and conspiratorial ways. They can be like poison darts thrown in the darkness. They injure, pain and take great tolls on their victims. This pain frequently causes a violent response.

Violent behavior is a reflection of extreme anger toward self and humanity. The ill feelings of anger, resentment and revenge represent pain. The pain was produced by injustice. Violent behavior is an attempt to 1) Get rid of the pain. 2) Get rid of the source of the pain. 3) Share the pain to lessen its severity.

When painful and threatening acts are interpreted as being unjustified, the severity of the pain increases. The person harboring the anger, resentment and revenge may not be aware of the causes or the reason for these painful emotions. But they realize that they are hurting. The hurt is often too severe to bear alone. If they cannot find a specific person on which to place blame, they will place blame on humanity or people as a whole. They have this need to get rid of the pain. If they cannot get rid of the pain alone, they are compelled to share it with others. This accounts for a lot of misdirected aggression and blind violence. The victims of injustice, in seeking relief from their own misery, frequently, commit violence against innocent people.

What is this violence that fills people with venomous hatred? What is the human injustice that programs its victims for violence and self-destruction? To be without the basic necessities of life is violence. To be without hope is violence. To be without love is violence. The deprivation of justice is violence. Ignorance is violence. Unemployment is violence, to be hungry and without shelter is violence. Poverty is violence. To be helpless and misrepresented is violence. To be without liberty and freedom is violence. To be forced to live without human dignity is violence.

# CHAPTER 7

## The Pain Of Injustice

When it appeared to me that all of my positive, rational, and legal alternatives had been exhausted without results, I began to feel the severe pain of injustice. I felt that my best blows had been thrown and my wisest strategy used. I had utilized with maximum efficiency all of the human and spiritual resources at my disposal. I had painstakingly documented all the facts concerning my mistreatment during the course of my employment and my subsequent dismissal. As in the case of an experienced and confident checker player, I had made all the right and proper counter moves. I knew that right was in my favor. However, the non-merit system would not yield any beneficial results for me. The injustices continued and the pain increased.

In addition to the painful feelings of disappointment, disgust, and indignation, I felt the encroachment of the depress- ing feelings of helplessness and despair. I realized that this frightening feeling must not gain full admission to my consciousness. It must be warded off. I must not admit helplessness. To do so would be a state of panic in midstream. To panic in midstream is to drown. To drown would allow injustice to triumph. To drown would be the surrender of righteousness. Somehow, I felt that I must force myself to rise out of depression and despair and let the will of God be done in my life. This was my sincere desire, but as we shall see later it was beyond my power.

It was one evening in November 1975 following a judge's decision not to reinstate me to my job. I was unable to sleep. I arose quietly from my bed so as not to disturb my wife who was asleep. I had suffered a series of disappointments in trying to get justice. It seemed as if the poison darts of Satan started striking from all sides. It was unusual for me to awaken after midnight. It was unusual for me to experience difficulty going to sleep.

My mind started working frantically attempting to figure out the reasons behind the conspiracy that resulted in the dismissal from my job and the conspiracy preventing my reinstatement. Hundreds of questions started racing through my mind. How wide is the conspiracy? Who is involved? Who are my friends? Who are my enemies? How can the two be distinguished? How long will fragile friendships last? Who can be trusted? Who designed this unjust conspiracy? My mind went into a process of trying to examine and analyze all the voluminous questionable data every questionable word, statement, expression, and impression. My mind tried to figure out the puzzle without success. The missing links won't connect.

Realizing that my mental processes were speeding out of control, I made a conscious effort to divert my mind away from this unbearable intensive mental activity brought on by audacious and inhuman injustice.

Injustice was not new to me. I consider myself a veteran warrior in coping with injustice. I was born and reared in the Deep South in the decades of the 1940s and 1950s. I had seen and experienced injustice in its worst forms. However, on this particular night, I found myself unable to cope with the accumulated pains of injustice.

In addition to the long months of unrelenting struggle for justice, I developed an immediate and urgent problem. That problem was an overstimulated brain. The overstimulation of the sensory perceptions of my brain magnified and exaggerated all the thoughts that flowed through my mind. Multi-trades of ideas, on their own, continued to explode in my imagination, stimulating my brain beyond its capacity to cope. Sleep would not come. I was in a state of perpetual restlessness. It seemed as if my mind had gone haywire. It was analogous to an automobile standing still with its engine running at full blast with no key to turn it off and no way to slow it down.

My mind was tormented by the sting of injustice. The painful thought of injustice brought continuous shock to my central nervous system. My brain was overworked, unregulated, and disoriented. The endless succession of ideas exploding in my brain was out of my control. I could not stop or regulate them. The internal universe of my mind was in chaos. My internal world was threatened with catastrophic collapse. It seemed that the stars of my universe were falling in all directions. They were colliding and exploding.

As I feared for my own well-being, the fear itself increased the malfunctioning of my brain. During this hyper-excitement state, my brain was sending out uncontrolled impulses. I feared that my brain would send lethal messages. Some could be suicidal or homicidal. I feared that my lungs might be told to collapse or my heart to stop beating. I feared shock, stroke, and delirium tremens. I feared that the intense nondirected mental activity might burn up my brain or cause a cranial explosion.

All of my psychic energy seemed directed toward this one all-consuming subject of my personal victimization. It seemed that I had no power to change the direction of my thinking. I tried in vain to think of something else. I was familiar with all of the literature on positive thinking. I read my favorite beauty spots in the Bible about faith, hope, and love. I prayed to the almighty God. I tried everything I knew to defuse the painful mental pressure on my mind. But the ugliness surrounding my mistreatment was too overpowering to be denied or shut out. My mind was obsessed with an unregulated compulsion to search for clues that would help to answer the questions of my predicament. I prayed for a ray of light out of this darkness. I prayed for mercy, sleep, rest and peace. They were delayed and would not come.

I found myself witnessing my own personal nightmare. It was accompanied by an overwhelming fear. It was a real nightmare. It was happening while I was wide awake. I wished that it was a dream. But it was not. This nightmare was real. I feared for my sanity. I feared for my life. My bedroom was transformed into a "Garden of Gethsemane." I thought about the bitter cup that confronted Jesus when he said in Matthew and Mark, "My soul is exceeding sorrowful, even unto death." Luke 22:44 says, "And being in agony he prayed more earnestly: and his sweat was as it were great drops of blood falling down to the ground." For the first time in my life, I received some insight into the painful dilemma of Jesus as he prayed three times for the bitter cup to be removed. It was the pain of depression and the hurt of unrelieved heartbreak. Why this brazen assault on innocence? Who can justify the betrayal of innocent blood?

My brain was running out of control, but my body conformed to contained behavior due to years of responsible conditioning. I also attribute this behavioral containment to safeguarding against further mental pain. In the face of not knowing what to do, I realized that irresponsible behavior can and often does cause more mental pain. So, I found myself mentally energized and behaviorally immobilized.

I could not find sufficient answers to make sense of my predicament. Consequently, I could not find a rational channel through which to ventilate or focus this overload of psychic energy. I found myself in the painful dilemma of being unable to slow down my mental processes, unable to act, and unable to sleep.

When the body is tired one can sit or recline and give it rest. But what about a racing mind that cannot get away from the obsession of ceaseless mental activity? It seemed that my frantic mental search for answers was futile. But the compulsion to search was uncontrollable. No answer was available. And yet it seemed as if my already overworked brain must have an answer before it would rest.

The pain of injustice overloads overstimulates, overworks, and overstrains the mental capacity of the mind. My mind was bombarded with the flow of endless data seeking constant and instant analysis for some clue of understanding and direction.

When the pain of injustice persists, the mind becomes afflicted with paranoia. It means that nothing can be trusted. All details must be examined. All motives must be questioned. The thousands of details that we accept by faith or take for granted normally, must now be examined. I became suspicious of anything considered unusual. The mind can no longer depend on the support of the environment. It depends on its limited and inadequate self. The task of examining the infinite details of one's environment is too great for a finite mind.

The paranoid person's external and internal environment is invaded by a multitude of objects characterized by suspicion and distrust. The mental processes of the brain overwork themselves in trying to identify and assess these enemy objects. It is a boring and depressing job because the mind abhors trivia and insignificant work. It is like a frantic search through a thousand haystacks in search of a needle. You realize that the needle is not worth looking for, but it could be the missing link that explains the puzzle. It could be the key that will unlock the door to the conspiracy. So, the mind must continue its search through haystacks of trivia. It no longer has time or energy to pursue more satisfying interests or goals. It must now respond to the emergency of taking care of itself. Nothing must be overlooked. Everything must be screened and scrutinized.

Some of the paranoid questions that I raised were: Has the bio-chemical nature of my brain been tampered with? Is it a chemical imbalance in my brain? Is it my mind? Have I been drugged? Is it the inside or outside world that's causing my mental crisis? Is this a nervous breakdown? Am I losing my sanity? Is my food or drink poisoned? How are they getting to my mind? Am I being manipulated?

My paranoid feelings suggested that not only were persons out to get me, but also, "something," or an unknown being. The paranoia suggests that the unknown being is aware of the effects of the injustice. The paranoid person gets the feeling that he is being watched. Worse than that he feels that his feelings and fears are known by the conspirator. It is a panicky and infuriating feeling that someone is trying to destroy your mind or drive you insane. The idea of deliberate injury to the mind raises more resentment and outrage than does deliberate injury to the body.

The paranoid person has a terrifying feeling that his thoughts are being read and his feelings known. The invasion of privacy is not just a matter of thinking that one's telephone is tapped, or his house or car is bugged, or that someone is watching. The matter is much more serious than this. It is the terrifying feeling that one's feelings and thoughts are exposed to the enemy and that there is no place to hide. It is the feeling that the ultimate privacy of the mind is invaded. It is a feeling that the enemy is aware of your feelings and is controlling the way you feel. It is a feeling that your struggle is not against, "flesh and blood, but against principalities and spiritual wickedness." These thoughts are accompanied by an overwhelming fear that borders on the edge of panic and despair.

The severe pain of injustice causes disorientation. Disorientation brings about a confused state. The person is diverted from his goals. His outward thrust is curtailed. The disoriented person loses a sense of direction. He does not know which way to go. To lose a sense of direction is to lose the ability to distinguish North from South and East from West, and up from down. A mentally disoriented person is lost in space, time, and circumstances. He loses touch with reality and with himself. He is unaware of his actions in relation to the outside world. It is to break harmony with the ordered universe. It is to lose step with the procession of life. It is to lose the rhythm of living. It is oblivion to one's surroundings. It is internal mental chaos.

The pain of injustice causes one to be surrounded by a cloud on a sunny day and causes dizziness without intoxicants. It blurs the vision of healthy eyes. It dulls the senses and distorts reality. It sets the brain on fire and breaks the heart into a thousand pieces.

The disoriented person loses a sense of priority. To lose a sense of priority is to lose the ability to make enlightened choices. Choices and decisions become random and arbitrary. When one cannot distinguish priorities his mind is indecisive, and his actions are imunobilized or misguided. The pain of injustice clouds our minds and causes us to stumble in darkness.

It is said, "It is easier to go out and meet danger than it is to wait for it." But where does one go and what does one do when he cannot distinguish priorities? How can he go out and meet danger when he does not know where it is or what it is? Perhaps it is that indecisive waiting that is a part of the pain. The dreadful anticipation as to what injustice will happen next and why it happened in the first place, plagues the mind.

The pain of injustice causes the mind to become deregulated. The equilibrium of the human organism is lost. When the mind loses its natural ability to regulate itself a major crisis is precipitated in the life of that person.

The mind is the person's regulating mechanism, What happens when the human regulator becomes unregulated? It can no longer regulate the body effectively. Therefore, the body is neglected and suffers. The energies of the mind are diverted to itself for its own well-being and survival. When the mind is compelled to consciously start taking care of itself, the organism becomes a "house divided against itself. The unity of the organism is destroyed. The primary components of the individual, his body and mind, have lost their mutuality. They do not function as a harmonious unit as before. They have lost their wholeness. They are out of tune with each other. The mind, body and spirit suffer.

The pain of injustice bypasses the body and afflicts itself in the mind or the psyche itself. It causes direct mental conflict. Outward behavior may not accurately reflect the severity of mental pain suffered by the victim of injustice. The pain of injustice is a direct assault on the victimized person as distinguished from the body. Assault against the body is one thing. Assault against the mind is something else.

The pain of injustice is designed to cause the person to self-destruct from internal pressures. The lethal explosives and pai sons somehow lodge themselves in the mind. Their symptoms are anger, resentment, depression and rage. These emotionally charged feelings are internally destructive. The pain of injustice does not require physical contact with the victim. It requires only the painful realization that someone has done you wrong. These bitter, unpleasant thoughts generate toxins that poison the body. Injustice is contaminated with germs of destruction. It is painful to realize that another human being, a member of the human family, could be so unfair and uncaring that he could mistreat another human being with such utter disregard. It is shocking to our sensibility to realize that man, the prize of God's creation could deviate so far from the will and images of God. It is shocking and unreal to learn that someone you have known to be a decent citizen is really a criminal in disguise.

The hurt mind and suffering brain which have previously taken care of the needs of the body now finds itself threatened and in urgent need of protection. There is a fear that internal resources have been exhausted without finding a sufficient defense. The fear is accompanied by an awful and crushing feeling of helplessness. It is a feeling that there is no longer sufficient resources to cope with the impending problem. It is a powerlessness that says you cannot solve the problem or save yourself. There is a fear that if you fail the forces of injustice will be encouraged to crush you and all the imps in Hell would rejoice. Out of the midst of your exhaustion and despair, you are still crying out that injustice must not win! The thought that injustice might win increases the mental pain. In- justice must not win!

It is a feeling of being overwhelmed with the world closing in around you. There is no place to escape, not even in the "foxhole" of the mind. There is no space in the brain to hide. It is a feeling of mental entrapment. The internal mentality is so disturbed that there is no place to sleep or rest. Depression is coming. Where can I run? Where can I hide? Where can I find rest? The persevering mind refuses to give up its frantic search for these and other urgent needs. The overworked and overstimulated brain continues on its own.

During this mental crisis, I felt the need for a pacer to regulate my mind. It was like an untuned engine of an automobile idled too high. It was backfiring, skipping and misfiring. The motor races wildly but the automobile is not moving. The over-stimulated brain is a racing of motor with the gears of the mind in neutral. Excessive energy is utilized with no movement or productive actions. If only a decision could be made as to what direction to travel, some of the tension and outrage would be defused. This would give the energy outward focus and perhaps reduce the activity of my overstimulated brain.

How does one fight the mental pain of injustice? There are anti-toxins and antibodies to fight off germs that attack the physical body. When the physical body is attacked by germs, disease and injury the antibodies go to work to destroy the foreign agents. There is a need for antibodies against the pain of injustice.

The depression was like a hammer striking crushing blows to my mind. The excruciating pain was unbearable. But at last, I knew the name of this malady, this toxic poison, this lethal germ and crippling disease. Its name is injustice. Its damages are real. It is a killer of democracy. It is a killer of people, their hopes and dreams.

There is an urgent need for immediate relief from the pain of injustice. This need is not recognized by most agents responsible for administering justice. The reason the need for im- mediate relief is so urgent is because of the severe pain, damaging effects and the potential for violence.

Continued stress, anxiety and depression can and often do cause physical and mental illness. The unrelieved pain of injustice is not only a health hazard but also life-threatening. It often contributes to crime and violence. An injury to the mind can be as serious as an injury to the body. The pain of injustice is real. Unless the pain is relieved the damages get progressively worse. Injustice triggers feelings of outrage, disgust, anger, resentment, depression and vengeance. These painful feelings can be devastating to the mental, emotional, physical and social health of the victims. The pain can reach such severe levels of intolerance that the person is compelled to vent his feelings, usually in some forceful or violent manner.

A forceful or violent act offers an immediate release of explosive energy. This gives relief from the pain even if it is temporary relief.

The literature and other news media are replete with numerous instances of forceful and violent actions by individuals who feel that they have been treated unjustly. Some have marched, picketed, and boycotted in protest. Some have assaulted or shot their supervisors and others feel responsible for their mental pain. Some have hijacked planes and buses. Some have committed suicide in such extreme manners as setting aflame their gasoline-soaked bodies. Some have committed violent crimes of vengeance. Some have committed homicides against members of their own families. These violent actions are indicative of the extreme pain and pressure of internal rage produced by the pain of injustice. It highlights the extreme human destructibility of injustice. This is not to suggest that all forceful and violent actions are caused by the pain of injustice. However, large numbers of people resort to violence to get immediate relief from intolerable mental pain.

I am convinced that many victims of injustice commit homicides to safeguard their sanity. They kill while temporarily in- sane, to prevent prolonged insanity. Injustice seems to have a profound effect on the body chemistry of many of its victims. The central nervous system is affected the most. nervousness, insomnia, blackouts, recent memory loss and dizziness are some of the symptoms. The victim of injustice frequently becomes irresponsible, and susceptible to strokes, seizures and heart attacks. He may become neurotic or psychotic, a criminal or drug abuser. These are negative options that are chosen to lessen the pain of injustice. Injustice hurts the mind. It breaks and daggers the heart. It destroys enthusiasm and mutilates the spirit. The administration of justice and people generally, have not begun to recognize this killer of people and their dreams. Society offers some relief for broken-down bodies, but what about relief for broken-down minds?

My need for immediate relief was ignored. Justice was to continue to be delayed indefinitely. The fact that I had sought relief in the proper place designated by the highest laws of the land and the fact that my case was in the breast of the courts, and I still could get no justice increased my pain. The frustrations and pressures reached an intolerable level. The delay or denial of justice amounts to additional injustice.

As the mental anguish and excruciating pain continued, I developed an urgent need to make some crucial decisions and to take some drastic actions with immediacy. I was compelled to seek immediate relief from this pain.

It is noted that I reached this point of desperation after a long process of legitimate strivings. I had exhausted all positive, rational and legal alternatives. All of my legitimate strivings had been unprofitable, and even painful. I had exerted my maximum effort in the pursuit of justice. But each time it eluded my grasp. How painful it is to witness the legal process of justice turn into, before your very eyes, the illegal process of injustice? It is shocking, disappointing and terrifying.

At this point, seeking justice was no longer the primary objective. Seeking relief from mental pain becomes the primary objective. Ordinary remedies to achieve this are no longer sufficient. They had been tried. Only extraordinary remedies will be sufficient to relieve the pain. The internal rage is so painful that it must be released immediately or explosively. It seeks to explode against others. It seeks to explode against self. To withhold the explosive rage longer would be to threaten the central nervous system with a mental breakdown, shock, delirium tremens and/or a deathly coma. What are the choices available to defuse the explosive rage? At this critical point, all choices for the relief of the unbearable pain must either be radical or violent as we shall see.

The possible remedies to satisfy the urgent need for relief from pain narrowed to six categories: (1) Give Up (2) Homicide (3) Suicide (4) Insanity (5) Rapid and prolonged drug tranquilization (6) A radical religious faith. All of these choices are painful. None offer a guarantee of satisfaction. All choices were risky. A choice must be made while I had the mental capacity to do so. The choices are difficult, but the pain compelled me to take some immediate course of action for some relief. The following were considered:

## 1. GIVE UP

I thought about giving up and saying to hell with it and turning my back on further attempts to get justice. If I give up maybe the pain will subside. If I give up maybe the pain from the numerous disappointments will ease. Because there can be no disappointment where there is no expectation. Maybe, if I stopped hoping for justice I would stop hurting from injustice. Most of my pain has resulted from the mutilation of my hopes and expectations for justice. Experience taught me that the higher the hopes the lower the despair. The greater the expectations the more severe the disappointments. The hopeful highs have been followed by depressive lows. Painful disappointments can make us afraid to hope. I don't want to be lifted high on the wings of false hope to be dropped low in the dark pit of despair. If uplifts are going to be followed by letdowns, it is preferable not to have the uplifts. Crashes are painfully shattering.

Therefore, giving up might help to escape from present pain and avoid future pain. Giving up was not an acceptable alternative because it would be abdicating responsibility as a citizen. It would be inexcusable passive acquiescence to intolerable wrong.

To give up would mean the abandonment of hope, pride and a righteous cause. Without pride, hope and a righteous cause, life would be robbed of much of its meaning. To give up in the face of injustice is an invitation for unrighteousness to continue roughshod, unchecked and without resistance. To give up is to embrace a false security. It is like going to sleep in a burning house. To give up would be to pretend that the injustice does not exist. It is tantamount to sanctioning wrong.

Giving up the strenuous struggle for justice would relieve the pain only in so far as I could pretend that it was not there or that it would go away. Therefore, giving up would be an attempt to deny the reality of the very thing that was causing me the most pain. It would be turning away from reality, life and truth. The intoxicating and tranquilizing effects of alcohol and drugs would not be powerful enough to make the mind forget the horrifying pain of this injustice.

Giving up is not an acceptable remedy for this pain.

## 2. HOMICIDE

I feared mental breakdown, insanity, delirium tremens, coma and death from the mental pain of injustice, I searched frantically for relief. As I sank deeper in pain I felt a homicidal vengeance against all those persons responsible for my pain. At several points, I felt that this would be the only way to safeguard against permanent damage to my psychological well-being. I felt a compulsion to strike out violently against those who had caused me this mental anguish. I felt that justice required punishment. I was placed in the painful dilemma of having to choose to save my sanity and my life by taking the lives of those responsible for my pain or allowing myself to go insane or die by letting them live. I felt that they were the criminals who had committed high crimes against me and my family. They are fugitives from justice. They must pay for their crimes. My relief from the mental pain depended on justice. I felt with absolute certainty that the death of the perpetrators would have relieved my pain.

It must be pointed out here that administrative justice had failed at my place of employment and with the county. Legal justice had failed in the courts. Moreover, justice had been deliberately circumvented. All other sources of help had been appealed to without results. Homicidal vengeance or the desire for violent retribution was not among the first choices.

My experience with mental pain forced me to revise my thinking about the notion of temporary insanity. I am convinced that there is such a mental state as temporary insanity. The temporary insanity is relieved by the violent act. If the insanity was not relieved by the violent act, it would be prolonged insanity or irreversible psychological damage or coma. Therefore, the violent act is an extreme effort of desperation to avoid insanity and relieve pain.

The pain of injustice compelled me to consider killing those persons who were responsible for my pain. It was a vengeful passion and compulsion that was overriding my will and rationality. I felt very strongly that their death would relieve my pain and save my sanity. Moreover, it appeared at certain points that their death or some other horrible misfortune would be the only thing that could relieve my pain and save my sanity. The pain was forcing me to choose between saving my sanity or taking their lives. The intensity of the pain could have very easily compelled me to choose the second alternative. The choice of homicide was held in abeyance contingent upon the intensity and duration of the pain. I was convinced that pain resulting from injustice can drive a person to kill. This made me realize the validity of temporary insanity. Violence committed during temporary insanity is a passionate and compulsive act to relieve mental pain. Homicide is a destructive alternative.

## 3. SUICIDE

Suicide is an alternative to extreme intolerable mental pain. It is more likely to be used when the victim of the pain cannot identify the source or because of his pain. Many times, a successful conspiracy can obscure the source. However, mental pain resulting from injustice is caused by other persons. Therefore, the victim of the pain seeks relief by striking out at life through others, even his own life.

The victim's pain arises out of injustice. He cannot accept the injustice that he has suffered. He cries out for justice as one man cries out for liberty. This desperate request is paraphrased as "give me justice or give me death." But because the victim feels a responsibility to avenge himself of the injustice, he holds on in an effort to survive the pain. I realized that to try to relieve pain by killing one's self is like jumping into the river to get out of the rain. I did not want to become an ally against myself. Suicide might relieve pain, but it would not bring justice.

The victimized person desperately wants two things: relief of pain and justice. It is perhaps that desire for justice that makes one hold on to life in spite of pain. Therefore, suicide was not an acceptable alternative. Suicide might end the pain, but it would not help the cause of justice.

## 4. INSANITY

Insanity is another radical alternative to pain and injustice. At certain points when the depression, hopelessness and panic became unbearable for me, I felt that a little faltering of the will would have plunged me into the irrational and unreal world of insanity. There was that temptation to block out the painful thoughts and unpleasant memories of the injustices perpetrated against me.

The more I thought about the injustices the more mental anguish I suffered. These thoughts, as unpleasant as they were, were documented reality. I was the victim of a conspiracy. I had been misrepresented. I had been robbed of a job. Worse, I had been denied justice by the Department of Justice. My whole way of life had been interrupted.

These were the realities. My mental dilemma was: How to cope with a reality that was too painful or how to retreat from the same reality that was too overwhelming. The crime against me was too painful to cope with and too overwhelming to forget. An extreme insanity would be required to bury such a wide magnitude of reality.

Withdrawal, isolation, bedsickness was tempting.

Many thoughts regarding the acts of injustice are so painful and so revulsive that they are psychologically indigestible. The reality of the unjust act is so revulsive it is sickening to think about. It cannot be contained within the psyche without a major disturbance and upset of mental balance. The unpleasant reality must change, or the person must take drastic and radical actions to change the reality or change himself. The injustice is so incompatible with one's inner feelings of equity that the two cannot be reconciled or coexist.

Insanity was tempting as an alternative because it offered some hope of relief from the mental tightrope walking. It takes an extreme amount of psychic energy to constantly put forth effort to keep from going insane. Mental control is usually a normal and automatic function. It is a burden when it becomes an urgent voluntary (required) effort. The temptation is to let go of this tedious mental control. To let go would mean the unleashing of pent-up rage. It would mean the ventilation of accumulated hurt. It would release some of the pain. It would mean giving up tightrope walking. Insanity was not chosen because it would be a reckless plunge into unreality. It would mean the relinquishment of responsibility. It is to give up one's autonomy. Sanity is a prerequisite to fighting injustice. Insanity might provide relief from pain. But it is a flight from reality and responsibility. It is an abandonment of care for one's self and future. To be- come insane is to become dependent on others. It is a regression from adulthood to infantilism. The war against injustice requires responsibility, adulthood, a sense of independence and sanity. Insanity is self-defeating.

## 5. DRUG SEDATION AND TRANQUILIZATION

The two primary functions of drugs are to kill pain and cause sleep. I was in need of both. But to kill pain and chemically induce sleep would be an irresponsible act that ignores the external causes of the pain. It would ignore the injustice. Sedation and tranquilization are the sleep of death.

## 6. RADICAL RELIGIOUS FAITH

Extreme pain requires an extreme remedy. Ordinary remedies are not sufficient to cope with extraordinary problems. When one's brain is on fire with overstimulation from the pains of injustice, the most extreme actions appear needed. It must be an action that sees beyond the pain. It must be a superior alternative. A superior alternative defuses the rage without destroying the victim.

Giving up, homicide, suicide, drugs and insanity are extreme alternatives to relieve extreme pain. However, because of their human destructiveness, they are inferior alternatives. They are inferior because they are motivated and limited by pain. Their primary goal is to eliminate the pain. However desirable and urgent it becomes to relieve the pain of injustice; the ultimate goal must not be limited to just the relief of pain. If the relief of pain becomes an end within itself, then, it follows that any extreme means will suffice for its elimination. In the place of coldhearted injustice, create conditions for the existence of humane social justice. A superior alternative must ensure human survival and righteous triumph. "What does it profit a man to gain the whole world and lose his soul?"

I chose a radical religious faith as a superior alternative. It is characterized by a scientific uplift and a spiritual outreach. This involves the maximum human effort to withstand pain and not choose an inferior alternative. It is the maximum human effort to maintain mental balance in the face of intolerable pain. It is active waiting for divine intervention. It was a risk taken in hope. It is maximum dependence on the help of God through the leap of faith.

During this night when my thought processes were running out of control, I was convinced that I must select an extreme alternative. Justice would have relieved my mental agony. It would have brought equilibrium to my runaway thoughts. Justice would have relieved the fears, the terror and the panic. Justice would have given me the needed security and tranquility to rest and sleep. Justice could have relieved this horrible nightmare that I experienced during my awakened hours. But justice was not available. I had diligently sought after justice, and it eluded me in every instance.

In the absence of justice and in the midst of a mental crisis only extreme options are left.

It is natural for a mind possessed with pain to become obsessed with means by which to relieve that pain. This obsession for relief by any means can make one more prone to select an extremely inferior alternative. An extreme action is probably warranted and necessary, but if the alternative is inferior it becomes self-defeating and destructive of human values. Inferior alternatives fail to look beyond the pain. The inferior alternatives do not have a future orientation. The pain of injustice seeks the defeat of its victim. The selection of an inferior alternative is an indication of that defeat. A person who is provoked to choose an inferior alternative assists in his own destruction. The urgent need to relieve pain heightens the probability of choosing an inferior alternative. When issues of life and death are involved, accompanied by pain, an extremely superior alternative is needed.

A superior alternative must be able to relieve the pain, seek justice and ensure human survival. Giving up, suicide, homicide, drugs and insanity do not fulfill the above objectives. A superior alternative does not seek escape into a world of unreality, self-extinction, blind passion, or sedation. A superior alternative does not seek a chemical solution to a social problem. A superior alternative does not seek to anesthetize the pain of injustice. Rather, it seeks to get rid of injustice which is the source of the pain. It seeks to repair the damages of horror and pain that compelled me to select an extreme option. The first five of the six options were either irresponsible or destructive or both. The sixth option was risky. There was no guarantee that this faith in God would rescue me. There was also that temptation for me to go out and get justice for myself by violent vengeance. But there was a force that res- trained me and a voice that said, "Trust God."

In trusting in God to rescue me, I waited. I waited with faith and hope. I decided to "stand the storm" that was raging inside of me. I decided to risk my health, my sanity and my life. I put them in the hand of God. I do not know whether this extreme mental terror attack lasted for one hour or two hours. But it seemed as if it would never end.

Spiritual phrases that I had heard since I was a child ran through my mind. They helped to sustain me. One such spiritual phrase was, "He might not come when you call him, but He will be on time."

I attribute my survival on that fateful night to God. I attribute my refusal to give up the struggle for justice to God. I attribute my refusal to resort to drugs or violence to God. I attribute my desire to hold on to my sanity to God.

I am convinced that because of the pain of injustice, violent and destructive acts against the self and humanity result.

# CHAPTER 8

## Mental Injury and Mental Pain are Real

The mental injury and pain of injustice are often more severe than physical injury. An injury to the mind is often more damaging than an injury to the body. The pain of injustice can impair a person's health just as disease and physical injury impair the body. It can be life-threatening and also fatal. However, there appears to be a gross lack of recognition of this invincible fact. There is usually no haste to apply first aid or treatment to the victim of injustice. Even worse, there is no adequate remedy at law. The American Legal System and Health Institutions do not give adequate recognition to mental injury and mental pain. There is a health remedy for a physically injured head and for otherwise physically abused bodies. There is also a legal remedy at law for physical and aggravated assault. On the other hand, innumerable abuses and assaults on the mind go untreated and unrecognized. Subsequently, the perpetrators of mental assaults usually continue their crimes unchecked and unaccountable.

If a person sustains a physical injury to his body, some type of medical treatment is immediately sought. If the injury results from the wrongful act of another person formal charges are filed. This is an indication of the great concern (and rightly so) for broken legs, arms and backs, pierced and lacerated flesh. But where is the concern for broken and lacerated minds, wounded and mutilated feelings? Justice crawls at a snail's pace for those who are injured by injustice. The reality of the pain of injustice is frequently ignored.

Injustice has a peculiar way of upsetting the mind as poisoned food upsets the stomach. The revulsive thoughts of the unjust acts are so sickening that they will not digest or assimilate into the mind without mental pain and disturbance. It is simpler to regurgitate toxic food from the stomach than toxic thoughts from the mind. The sickening mistreatment frequently results in depression, headache, insomnia, withdrawal, tension, mental confusion, dizziness, disorientation, blackouts, loss of appetite, paranoia and loose associations. All of these are in addition to heartache, and anxiety and impaired functioning.

I am convinced from my own experience that the chemical imbalance resulting from the stress brought on by the pain of injustice causes people to become violent to get relief. Numerous instances indicate that it is less painful to risk being killed or shot than it is to seethe in the pain of injustice.

Injustice deprives a person of his human rights and robs him of a significant value that inherently belongs to him. Human rights are sacred rights. They are inalienable and nonnegotiable. Any person who violates the human rights of another person acts without legitimate sanction and at his own risk. It is a painful realization that one would take it upon himself and violate the human rights of another person.

The higher the hopes the more painful the disappointments. The series of high hopes followed by disappointments became so painful that I feared to hope. The greater the hope the greater the hurt. My hopeful highs continued to turn into depressive lows. I learned that a person could stop hoping to safeguard against the pain of disappointment. And yet, where there is no hope there is pain.

To paraphrase a Biblical statement, "Where there is no hope the people perish." The punishing pain of disappointments, especially where there is legitimate hope, can teach people to be afraid to hope. Imagine the anguish and the contortion of the mind and spirit when hope itself becomes a pain!

I placed hope in the legitimate and traditional agencies and institutions to get legal justice. I had every reason to hope for justice because the administrative crimes committed against me were clearly in violation of the U.S. Constitution, recent U.S. Court decisions, the State Laws of Georgia, and the Civil Service Laws of Metro County. The violations were specifically documented with the best and highest evidence. With unmistakable truth, undisputed facts and evidence beyond a shadow of a doubt, how could justice not prevail?

But as I pursued justice my hopes were successively and progressively followed by disappointments. The Civil Service Board, the lawyers, the Courts and the Judges were disappointing. The EEOC, LEAA, ACLU, Labor Relations Board and the U.S. Department of Justice were disappointing. The local news media, politicians and County Commissioners were disappointed. Yes, even the so-called community leaders and religious leaders whom I thought I could depend on were disappointing.

It is infuriating without measure to be forced into a position to have to beg, buy or bargain for something that already belongs to you. I was placed in this position in 1975 when my employment rights and human rights were violated during the course of being robbed of my job.

I exhausted all of the administrative remedies. I engaged attorneys and went through the legal processes. But the wheels of justice would not turn in my favor. My hopes turned to despair. My pain turned to panic.

It is an abomination and a disgrace for any person to be placed in a position to have to beg, buy or bargain for justice or for something that is rightfully his. It is a serious indictment on any society or civilization when this state of affairs occurs. The Creator meant for justice to be as free as air and water. "Let justice run down as water and righteousness as a mighty stream."

Can anyone deny the truth of Psalm Twenty-four? "The earth is the Lord's and the fullness thereof, the world and they that dwell therein." Yes, there are those irreverent and audacious persons who deny by their crimes against others that there is a God and a Creator of Righteousness.

It is a strange, shocking and painful experience to see people you have known for six, eight and even twelve years, take OFF THEIR MASKS that they had been wearing all these years. At first I could not believe what I was seeing or hearing. I had the disillusioning experience of seeing people unveil themselves, the selves that heretofore had been hidden. It became very clear to me that I had mistaken facades for true faces, and pretenders for real people. It was a strange sensation to hear voices and words coming from the bodies of people I thought I once knew. Their open, flagrant and bold dishonesty was in such contradiction to my perception of them that it was beyond belief.

I became painfully aware that not only had I been among strangers and did not know it, but I was among, "ravening wolves dressed in sheep clothing." I was among the criminals who lied, stole and robbed. I mistook strangers for friends. I asked myself, "How could I have been so naive? How could I have been so blind and deceived all these years?"

Other painful experiences were in store for me regarding my co-workers of many years. I was surprised to learn that co-workers whom I had known for the entire period of time I had been at the Court, suddenly were fearful of associating with me. They started avoiding me as if I had a contagious disease. I was the same person I had always been. And yet, in a matter of days, they reacted to me in a totally different way.

They especially did not want to be seen with me by the administrators and certain other persons whom they felt might get the message back to the administrators. They felt intimidated and that possible reprisals would be taken against them by the mere association with me. I was shocked to learn how fragile and superficial job friendship can be. Their reactions to me were so strange that it seemed that an evil ventriloquist was speaking through the bodies of the people I thought I knew.

It became mind-boggling to learn so much about so many people in such a short period. This crisis brought out unbelievable revelations. The thieves stole and destroyed. The cowards lied and denied the truth. The hypocritical betrayed. The selfishly indifferent looked on from a distance and passed by on the other side. Those who were figureheads played games. The crisis brought out strange selves that had been heretofore hidden in the people I thought I knew.

The injustice of my employment reductions, misrepresentations and subsequent termination were bad enough, but the added burden of discovering that I was among people whom I did not know and that they did not care was an extra heavy mental and emotional weight. This weight was overwhelming and painful.

The mental assaults and job robberies were not done by persons unfamiliar to me or by an alien institution. They were familiar acquaintances for a number of years. It was an institution to which I had willingly given twelve years of prime time of my heart, mind, body and soul. They are the priceless constituents of life.

This was a robbery by persons who were benefactors of my labor, citizenship and taxes. It is analogous to having given one's hands and in turn, being robbed of one's legs by the one you gave the hands. This crime was done in a public tax-supported agency. It was done by persons who are sworn under oath to uphold the U.S. Constitution and be representative of the government of the people.

The actions taken against me and the subsequent denials of justice represented the government working against the people who support it. It worked against me. It has worked against countless others. It does so sometimes without the knowledge or consent of the elected and constituted authorities. How can the government be excused for not protecting its citizens from the atrocious crimes of injustice? How can the government be excused for not having some safeguards against its abuse against its citizens? How can the government be excused for not weeding out its representatives who misrepresent it and in the process commit crimes and make a mockery of justice and the Constitution? How long can this government afford such flagrant criminal misrepresentation?

The most intense pain for me was because the act of robbing me of my job was also an attack on my family. It was a deprivation imposed on my wife and thirteen-year-old daughter, other family members and friends. It was not my pain that caused the most suffering. It was the family's pain. It was the hurt in the eyes of my wife, daughter and mother that broke my heart and threatened my mental breakdown. It was this combined pain that compounded my suffering. To feel the pain that they felt for me increased the pain that I felt for them. To see the hurt and feel the anxiety of my thirteen-year-old daughter broke my heart into a thousand pieces.

How must I break this news to my disabled mother, re- tired and unemployed father? They were partially dependent on me. They needed my help. But now, I find myself victimized, unemployed and in need of help myself. It was not just a matter of being robbed of a job. Although at the time this crime took place, in August 1975, the country was amid the highest unemployment rate and the worst economic depression since the early 1930s. It was an outrageous violation. It was the continuous accumulative injustices that compounded my pain. And although these documented wrongs were in the breast of the Court and the U.S. Justice Department I could not get any relief.

My flesh was not torn or lacerated. No blood was shed. No physical assaults were sustained. But the pain could not have BEEN MORE SEVERE. My life could not have been more threatened. The pain was real. I felt the injury. It affected my whole life and well-being.

I reached out through every avenue of hope that I knew, They turned out to be blind alleys and dead-end streets. They were false remedies and subterfuges. These avenues turned out to be exploitive and deceptive fronts. The disappointments and misrepresentations were injurious, and they added to my pain.

Physical injuries to various parts of the body are relayed to the central nervous system and they register as pain. The mental pain of injustice does not have to be relayed or transferred. It resides in and afflicts directly the nervous system. The hurt is in the brain and the mind. The brain and the mind hurt. The pain is real.

# CHAPTER 9

## Acute Psychotrauma

The medical definition of the word, trauma, according to Webster, is an injury violently produced. In psychiatry, Webster states that it is an emotional shock that has a lasting psychic effect. Psycho, means, the mind or mental processes. Acute, is defined as being sharp and severe. Acute is also defined as critical and crucial. It reaches a crisis in a short time. A crisis is a state of urgency that forces a turning point. The definitions of the words associated with acute psychotrauma are provided to lay a foundation for the meaning of this subject. The thesis of this composition is that injustice is a major cause of acute psychotrauma that precipitates pain, violence and death.

Acute psychotrauma is an intolerable emotional pain and shock to the mind. It is turmoil in the brain. It is a psychological crisis. It is a mental emergency. It is an overstimulated nervous system. The mental processes are overwhelmed with too many stimuli to respond to. The mental and emotional sensation created by the stimulus of outrageous injustice is out of proportion and beyond the capacity of the mind to regulate and the brain to coordinate. The precipitating injustice is too elusive and too insidious to resolve. It is too disappointing to acknowledge, too diverse to confront and too heartbreak- ing to face. Acute psychotrauma is inescapable and unresolvable mental and emotional pain. If it were painful hands or feet you could cut them off, or eyes, you could pluck them out. But how do you separate yourself from your mind and feelings?

Acute psychotrauma is an imminently intimidated mind and threatened sanity. The imminently perceived threat to one's sanity is more outrageous and frightening than a threat to one's life. It is an outrageous thought to consider that someone would be so cruel that they would drive you insane. It triggers infuriation without measure. The infuriation plus the fear of losing your sanity becomes a most difficult and diabolical dilemma to struggle with. This awful feeling of fear and outrage makes one realize that psychological warfare is more vicious and painful than physical combat.

It is a terrifying feeling to realize that you are rapidly approaching the breaking point or a mental breakdown and that this impending breakdown is being engineered by individuals who are perpetrating injustice against you. You are being forced to acknowledge that your mind can no longer cope with the gravity and complexity of your dilemma. You have run out of answers. All resources have failed. All possible solutions have been exhausted. Nothing has worked. Every effort and every thought has been in vain. Hope is gone. Despair is mounting.

The paralyzing helplessness of psychotrauma is analogous to being in a state of animated suspension. You're walking nor your running bring you any closer to the place you are trying to reach. Your voice is not heard. Your visibility is not seen. Your feelings are not felt. Your strivings are unprofitable. Your significance as a member of the human race has vanished. The procession of life does not slow down or even take notice of your wounded condition on the roadside of life. Humanity is oblivious to the severity of your pain and the urgency of your needs.

The core of psychotrauma is a mental condition. Mental, according to Webster, means, with the mind. The mind is the seat of self-consciousness. Put another way, the mind is the seat of consciousness of self. It is the sacred, private, personal and exclusive temple where the "I" and "me" and "myself" reside. Acute psychotrauma has a way of invading and disturbing the private domain where the self-resides. The traumatized person perceives a threatening enemy, not against his body, his life, or his property, but against his innermost self. He can withstand the bullets, sticks, and stones that attack his body and threaten his life. But the invisible darts that penetrate the core of his mind are more difficult to fight and struggle against because the fight is perceived as not against "flesh and blood," but against an evil and wicked conspiracy whose malevolent intent is to destroy the mind through mockery and a reign of malicious terror. It is frightening and humiliating to have to run and hide one's body from terroristic threats and attacks. The fear and humiliation are multiplied and transformed into outrageous indignation when it becomes necessary for the self to run and attempt to hide mentally. The most terrifying aspect of the acute psychotraumatic experience is discovering that there is no foxhole or hiding place, even in the mind. The feeling of mental entrapment brings the traumatized victim to the brink of insanity.

A sound mind and healthy brain oversee and protect the interests of the human organism. Messages from the mind and the brain regulate the systems of the body. The body has many systems. Some of the primary systems are: The central nervous system, the circulatory system, the respiratory system, reproductive system, the digestive system and others. In addition to regulating the systems of the body, the mind and the brain regulate human conduct.

They give directions in carrying out psychological, physiological and sociological functions. This brief background information is provided to establish a foundation for exploring the question: What happens to the human functioning of the body when the mind and brain are traumatized?

The mind usually and normally focuses outwardly, or outside of itself. It usually directs the functioning and activities of the body for comfort, security and future interest. It is a sensor and monitor of all of our internal feelings, sensations and bodily changes. It also focuses outside of the body and monitors and interprets all happenings in the external environment. It has an ongoing job of analyzing and synthesizing all internal and external stimuli and data. The mind performs all of this intricate work without focusing, obsessively, upon itself.

Therefore, it is a very extraordinary circumstance that causes the mind to turn inwardly on itself as a focus. Acute psychotrauma is one of those instances where the mind is forced to try to safeguard and take care of itself. It does so by directing most of the psychic energy upon itself. The mind becomes preoccupied with thoughts of its own safety and ability to withstand the perceived threats against itself. To imagine or contemplate the failure of one's own mind increases fear and depression. Because, in a real sense, if the mind collapses, the body and all its systems will fail. Not only will the body fail, but the "I" and the "me" and "myself" will fail. It would represent a total defeat of my life by an evil enemy using the weapon of injustice. The burden of survival is placed on a mind that is under fierce attack itself.

When the mind starts concentrating its psychic energy within itself, the process of withdrawal begins, and other parts of the body and other areas of life suffer. This withdrawal process impacts physiologically, psychologically, socially and spiritually. They suffer because there is an emergency in the mind. And all of the available psychic energy has been summoned to rescue the mind.

Physiologically speaking, it is not unusual for the victims of psychotrauma to have their vital signs elevated with high blood pressure and a more rapid pulse rate. They may become dizzy and experience headaches, numbness and other unusual sensations about the head. Frequently, there is a loss of appetite and sleep disturbance. Palpitation of the heart and shortness of breath may occur. The body takes on a stiffness. The usual flexibility and spontaneity of the body become substantially reduced. There exists a general tiredness, although physical activity has been decreased. Unexplainable pains and psychosomatic ailments often develop. Interest in personal grooming, household chores and routine activities around the house declined. I feel certain that during this withdrawn and traumatic condition that the major systems of the body are in states of disequilibrium. The major inclination of the body is to decline and recline. Physical activity becomes more and more curtailed.

The excessive mental preoccupation causes social withdrawal. There is very little energy to maintain contact with friends and relatives. The traumatized person withdraws from the meetings and clubs and even the church that he usually attends with regularity. He stops calling friends and relatives. When he gets calls, his conversation is usually short. He forces himself to try to sound and act normal. He will make some excuses to terminate the conversation as soon as possible. He withdraws to his own house, usually, in the bedroom or some corner to be alone with his painful thoughts. Although physical and social activities have been sharply reduced, mental activity has accelerated.

The concentration of excessive psychic energy in the mind and the brain creates a mental inferno. This tormenting hell within the mind is the very core of the acute psychotraumatic experience. It represents a mind struggling and fighting to save itself from the demonic forces of injustice. It represents a mind that has called upon all of its internal resources to defend itself from an invasion of evil. The high concentration of energy pressurizes the mind. It becomes a painful overheated mental compression chamber. In its desperation to find answers and solutions to relieve the pain of injustice, the brain becomes overworked. The brain becomes a malfunctioning computer, running out of control in search for the elusive parts to a malicious and lethal conspiracy. The restless, compulsive and obsessive mind has programmed the brain to search everywhere possible and everything conceivable to find the answer. The brain is further programmed to search with urgency because time is running out and the pain is already unbearable.

The alert and conscientious brain attempts the impossible task of examining and analyzing an endless array of data in the environment. Everything and everybody must be checked out for any clue or any evidence of the grand conspiracy. Every action must be analyzed. Every motive must be questioned. No one can be trusted. The expressions on their faces must be studied, their smiles, their laughs and their tone of voice. Their gestures, their silence and even the things that they don't say must be scrutinized and suspect. The questions become endless without answers. And, yet the brain continues its urgent search, rapid analysis and frantic examination of every questionable thing within its grasp.

As the brain escalates to its maximum operational level, strange and frightening things begin to happen. There is a realization that the brain is overworked and is at the breaking point. And the consequences of the breakdown of an overloaded and overworked brain are unknown and frightening. But there is a feeling in the traumatized cranial explosion and a mental collapse and death. The very fear itself, of a breakdown, seems to add to the escalation and workload of the brain. The brain is running out of control. It is overstimulated. The mind raises the question, "How can I slow down my brain?" There appears to be no power within to slow down the brain. The imagination becomes lively. The mind appears to be a world within itself. Thoughts and ideas are very vivid, some can be seen and heard. They form and fade. Some thoughts race through the mind on their own.

Parenthetically speaking, this is the most frightening and most crucial aspect of psychotrauma. This is the point where drastic and violent actions frequently take place. The traumatized victim commits violence in a desperate attempt to turn off the frightening tapes running through his mind. He commits violence to draw attention to the pain of injustice. He commits violence to return from his world of insanity. He commits violence to escape the entrapment of his mental obsession and psychological isolation. He commits violence to avoid spontaneous self-destruction. He commits violence to create a less frightening and less painful reality. He commits violence to bring an end to a nightmare that was not in his wildest dreams.

The most urgent need for the acutely traumatized mind is relief. Relief from the fears, pressures and pain precipitated and sustained by injustice. The traumatized mind needs relief from the mental abuse and psychological assaults from the poison daggers of injustice. The severe shock and injury to the traumatized mind are just as real as a bullet to the head. Acute psychotrauma is often as fatal as a bullet to the head. Injustice can precipitate acute psychotrauma.

# CHAPTER 10

## Justice:
## A Vital God-Given Human Right

Justice is a vital human right. It is vital because it is an indispensable human need. There is something in the human psyche that cries out for that which is right, fair and just. When this human need for justice is not met or when one is deprived of justice, a type of suffering or human deficit is created. It causes a negative reaction and a deficit in the human potential. In other words, it takes away something that is needed for normal human functioning.

God has elevated justice as a foremost priority in governing the relationships among human beings. It is his way and requirement for all mankind. In the first book of the Bible, Genesis, chapter 18, verse 19, justice is proclaimed as the way of the Lord: "And they shall keep the way of the Lord, to do justice and judgment." The book of Deuteronomy, chapter 16, verse 20, makes a similar admonition, "That which is altogether just shalt thou follow, that thou mayest live, and inherit the land which the Lord thy God giveth thee."

The prophet Micah, chapter 6, verse 8, is even more explicit about the requirement of justice: "doth the Lord require of thee, but to do justly, love mercy and walk humbly with thy God." The fact that God requires human beings to be just, such requirement creates a human right for every person to receive justice. Therefore, justice is not merely a human right, but it is a divine right ordained and sanctioned by God.

Justice is the uncompromising and unchanging law of God. Proverbs, chapter 11, verse 1, describes God's position most succinctly, "A false balance is an abomination to the Lord: but a just weight is his delight." When the requirement of justice is not met, there are also detrimental consequences for injustice.

## HUMAN JUSTICE OUGHT TO EXIST NATURALLY

God has created natural laws that govern the physical environment and the universe. These laws enable plants and animals to live. These laws regulate all movement, change and balance. He has created a 360-degree circle and a 180-degree straight line. He has created a non-arbitrary point where the measurement of a level surface can be achieved. God has laws governing the freezing and boiling points of water and other substances. He has laws governing the chemical composition of matter, and the speed of light and sound. These natural laws make it possible for physical scientists to experiment, plan, invent, manufacture and build. Just as God has natural laws, God also has moral and social laws. Social justice is an inescapable moral law.

Justice is a basic and primary human need. Being deprived of justice is like being deprived of water when you are thirsty, food when you are hungry and oxygen when you are suffocating. Even worse, it is like substituting vinegar for water to quench thirst and stones for bread to satisfy hunger. It is like being given a crown of thorns to shield one's head from the heat of the burning noonday sun. The extreme deprivation of justice is designed to force one to participate in his crucifixion by compelling him to carry the cross on which he is to be hanged.

Justice as a vital human need is recognized by all major world religions. It is recognized as such by all civilized societies. Justice is the primary reason for the development of laws and governments: Many of the governments of the world, as does the United States Government, have a Department of Justice. The U.S. Government has multiple administrations of justice.

There are Courts of Law and justices of the peace throughout the land. There are complex judicial systems in every state and segment of government with the responsibility of administering justice. The chief purpose of a democratic government is to ensure justice for all of its people. The importance of justice is in most literature of the world. The human need for justice has been well-documented since the beginning of civilization. The documentation of the need has been accepted. However, the practice of this creed has been grossly neglected.

## HUMAN JUSTICE OUGHT TO BE FREE

Justice is a balance of the scales of human rights. It is an equitable distribution of what is rightfully due to each individual. These dues are not limited to material goods alone. The apostle Paul sums up what is due others in Romans 8:7 through the 8 verse, by saying, "Render therefore to all their dues: a tribute to whom tribute is due; custom to whom custom; fear to whom fear; honor to whom honor. Owe no man anything, but to love one another; for he that loveth another hath fulfilled the law."

Those who commit injustice against others are indebted to their victims. They owe them for taking away something that was not their due. How great must be the debt of those who practice injustice!

Love and mercy can do more than justice. But they can never do less. Love is a Savior. It rescues. It redeems. It gives unconditionally. Love and mercy give values of goodness in addition to justice. Love goes beyond the balance of justice and gives that which is not deserved or rightfully due. Justice is the even breaking point where nothing is given, and nothing is taken. Love does not exclude justice, but it goes beyond justice.

Love is not subtraction. It is an addition. On the other hand, anything less than justice is injustice. Goodness that goes beyond justice is love and mercy. Injustice represents a subtraction that creates a deficit. It is the taking away of something that be- longs to someone else. Injustice is a human rights violation that deprives a person of a vital human need.

It must be pointed out that most human rights violations are not illegal, and therefore, beyond the protection of Statutory Law. There are innumerable ways to mistreat people and be unfair to them without breaking any Federal, State, or Municipal laws.

Unrighteousness and injustice manifest themselves in a multitude of forms and fashions that are not covered by statutory law. There is a popular saying that "Morality cannot be legislated." This saying has much validity. Legislation can and does help in preventing and adjudicating overt acts that violate the law, but it has little influence on covert acts of injustice. Injustice perpetuates itself in many clandestine forms. It is a characteristic nature of injustice to mask and cloak itself in disguises of deception. There is much adeptness in committing wrongs that cannot be proved to violate the law.

Injustice often finds a way of circumventing prosecution and accountability even when a statutory law has been violated. The pursuit of justice in our sophisticated judicial system is very elusive and expensive. Too frequently, the cost of justice in the courts exceeds the cost that gave grounds for legal action.

There is something unjust about paying for justice. And there is something wrong when the cost for justice in the courts costs more than the injustice that brought the case to court in the first place. And yet, it is not unusual for plaintiffs seeking justice in the courts (and sometimes defendants) to spend strenuous efforts, long years, thousands of dollars, and suffer traumatic disappointments and unbearable stress without any relief in the unending litigation process.

The very fact that many people are willing to pay more to get justice than the cost of the injustice suffered, is a clear indication of that human need for justice. It is not just a need to balance material goods. It is a need for spiritual and psychological vindication. It is a need to resolve conflict in interpersonal relationships by flushing out the polluting causes.

Justice is an urgent need. It is pursued so relentlessly to eliminate the omnibus and audacious threat to the life, integrity and dignity of the human personality. Justice is needed to rid one's self from the nuisance of nagging old businesses so that a new agenda for living can begin. Justice is needed to bring an end to a captivation of feuding and fighting to be free to live again. To be free to live again explains why the victims of injustice are willing to pay a great price for justice.

There is a vital need for justice in all human transactions. This simply means that in the course of our dealing with each other, we must not take from another that which does not be- long to us. This is the essence of the Golden Rule, "Do unto others as you would have them do unto you." The Golden Rule applies to all human transactions, from person to person, group to group, race to race, and nation to nation. The sources of conflict, violence, war and death can often be traced to violations of the Golden Rule.

Justice is so vital to the needs of human beings and society that it ought to be free. Justice ought to be free! We should not have to pay for it, beg for it, or bargain for it. Justice is a human right. Everybody is entitled to it. Even the people who practice injustice want to be treated justly, even lovingly. The very covert actions used to cover up injustice by those who practice it are an acknowledgment that justice is right. Their attempts to hide injustice or call it by another name is an acknowledgment that injustice is wrong and abhorred by the bright light of civilization.

## DEVICES TO CIRCUMVENT JUSTICE

Those who practice injustice continue to devise elaborate schemes to hide their wrongs and attempt to justify their actions. They often develop a labyrinth of complex laws, rules, regulations, policies, and procedures. Ironically, they are not always developed to assure justice but to provide loopholes to circumvent justice.

Many legal political and administrative devices have been invented to conceal justice and provide a hiding place for those who perpetrate injustice. They hide behind legal technicalities, arbitrary decisions, arbitrary motions, summary judgments, judicial immunity and statutes of limitations. A high number of case laws originating in appellate courts are frequently used viciously and arbitrarily to deny justice. So often, administrative and judicial decisions are not made according to what is right or wrong or just or unjust, but they are made on the basis of the latest appellate court decision.

Attempts to conceal injustice are frequently accomplished by indefinite court delays, compromising plea bargaining and backroom deals. Political expediency, greed for profit and moral cowardice frequently dictate decisions of injustice. False administrative remedies, judicial discretion, interlocutory conspiracies and unending litigation are often employed to deny that vital human right, called justice. All too often, human justice is denied by the so-called, administration of Justice.

# EPILOGUE

## Justice is Needed for Balance

Justice is that equitable force in human transactions that maintains an even balance in the exchange and distribution of values. These exchanges and distribution of values are characterized by mutuality and reciprocity that award each individual what he is rightfully due. The equitable force of justice works to restore equilibrium when the exchanges and distribution of values get out of balance. It is the balance and the equilibrium, which are universal, that suggest that justice is right and is in the best interest of society.

The phenomenon of justice, as it relates to balance, is interwoven with the natural environment. Balance in nature is a most conspicuous characteristic. It involves symmetrical forms, blending patterns and relationships. The limbs and branches of a tree spread out in even forms from the trunk that supports them. The spreading of the roots in the ground has a complimentary relationship to the spreading of the branches above the ground.

The fruit trees and vegetable plants distribute their produce in such a way as to provide balance. Apples, oranges, pears, grapefruits and peaches are so situated on the trees as to provide balance. Ears of corn, tomatoes, okra, peppers, beans and peas distribute themselves on the stalks on which they grow to provide balance. Balance spreads the weight more evenly.

There is balance in the sunshine and the rain. The rain does not come down in disproportionate gushes from the sky.

It does not come down in pints, quarts or gallons. It comes down in proportionate streams of droplets. The droplets give a balance and blend with the falling of rain. Just as there is a balance to the falling of rain, there is a balance in the shining of the sun.

The sun radiates an even flow of light and energy. Its light travels in a straight line, emanating in every direction. Every object within its path receives its benefit. A balance of sunshine and rain is essential to the life of plants and animals. Too much rain without the heat of the sun will bring about floods. Too much sunlight without the rainfall will bring about the droughts.

The creator has seen fit to provide a balance between the sunshine and the rain. This balance makes living, not just more favorable, but also, possible. In describing the love, goodness and justness of God, the Gospel of Matthew, chapter 5, verse 45, states thusly, "for he maketh his sun to rise on the evil and the good, and sendeth rain on the just and on the un- just." There is a broadness in God's mercy and a balance in his justice. This truth is revealed by the wet, weeping rainfall. It is declared by the warm and smiling sunshine.

It is true that some of the elements in nature indeed become unbalanced. This imbalance is demonstrated in hurricanes, earthquakes, tornadoes, volcanic eruptions, and floods. However, these conditions do not represent the norm. But when this imbalance does occur, there is another force operating to restore balance.

This force is known as the force of balance. It is built into the natural processes to regain and maintain equilibrium. The force of balance eventually tames the violent winds of the hurricane. The force of balance causes the earthquake to cease its ferocious trembling. It forces the erupting volcano to stop spewing its burning lava and spitting out its dragon fire. The force of balance is so strong that the violent twisting tornado can endure but for a short time. The dark clouds sometimes cover and obscure the clear blue sky. But the sunlight eventually breaks through and causes the clouds to vanish.

The stormy sea can be dangerously turbulent. But the force of balance brings an end to the raging storm and the waters become peaceful and calm. The thunder rumbles and roars. The lightning flashes its bolts of fire. But the force of balance silences the roaring thunder and extinguishes the fiery flashes of lightning. And once again the natural balance is restored.

A life-threatening situation can arise when the elements of nature get out of balance. This is illustrated by the Gospel of St. Mark, chapter 4, verses 37 through 39, when Jesus and his Disciples were in a storm at sea. Jesus was asleep. The raging storm compelled the Disciples to wake Jesus with the anxious question, "Master, carest thou not that we perish?" In response to their question St. Mark states, "And he arose, and rebuked the wind, and said unto the sea, peace, be still. And the wind ceased, and there was a great calm."

The Disciples were frightened because the climatic conditions had become unbalanced and had deviated from the norm and become disruptive and threatening. Jesus was called upon to bring the environmental conditions back to normal and re- store the climatic balance. There is a force to restore balance.

Balance is one of the most fundamental phenomena in the universe. The bodies of animals have bilateral symmetrical de- signs. Not only do they have a balanced design, but they have a system of maintaining balance during movement. Walking has been described as a process of falling from one foot and catching on the other. Walking and running involve a rhythm of losing and regaining balance. The respiratory system involves a balance between inhaling and exhaling. The circulatory system involves a rhythmic balance between heartbeat and heart rest.

The essential foundation of manmade structures is balance. In the construction of buildings, great care is taken to have a level foundation. The leveler is a most important tool in the building construction. The leveler, the compass, the square, the ruler and measuring scales are basic tools for building because their function is to assist in achieving balance. Balance is essential to the making of a chair, a watch, motor vehicles, a house, bridges and skyscraper buildings.

Balance is real. It is not an arbitrary manmade point or condition. It has a natural existence in the universe. In an effort to achieve maximum harmony and efficiency individuals must obtain the optimum balance. Balance is a basic goal of the scientist, the artist and the true religionist. The wheels and tires on motor vehicles must be round and balanced for efficient performance. Great music, paintings, sculpture and poetry must have balance. The true prophet seeks human justice for all people.

The universe is a cosmos, not chaos. It has order, unity, harmony, and continuity. The solar system that we live in is a unitary system of planets and moons that revolve around the sun. The planetary bodies have balanced structures. They travel with precision in designated orbits of their own. The universe contains constellations of galaxies and solar systems. This most fantastic design and order of the universe is the most remarkable phenomenon known to humankind. To the extent that man can observe and examine the universe, he finds structure, order and balance.

The fact that the heavenly bodies in the universe are not static, adds to the fantastic significance of cosmic balance. The universe is dynamic. It is alive with movement. Trillions and trillions of stars are shining. Trillions and trillions of planetary bodies are revolving and turning. Light is penetrating the dark voids of space at incredible speed. Infinite cosmic energy is being expended throughout the universe. Magnetic and gravitational forces are busy doing their work of magic unceasingly. And yet, in the midst of all of this dynamism of rhythmic infinity, THERE IS BALANCE IN THE UNIVERSE!

## BALANCE THE ESSENCE OF JUSTICE

The symbol for justice is the balanced scales. Justice is seen as having equal weight on either side. Balance is the essential characteristic of justice. Balance is abundant in nature. It is abundant in the universe. It is quite apparent that nature, the world and the universe are sustained by balance. The universe is in flux. Nothing is tied down. Constant change and movement are the characteristics of the universe. The universe is an incomprehensible miracle sustained by the divine force of balance.

Since balance is so pervasive throughout nature, the artifacts of civilization and the universe, it is only reasonable to conclude that balance must be pervasive throughout the society of human culture. When we think of balance in human relationships and social interaction, the word balance is translated into justice. Human justice is the fundamental balancing force in human relations and social interaction. If society is to maintain its balance, and if civilization is to survive, human justice must prevail. Injustice is an act of violence that leads to chaos and destruction.

Human justice is vitally needed for the healthy adjustment of the individual as well as for humans living collectively. Human justice is vital for the survival of the human race. Therefore, a new emphasis must be placed on human justice from the exclusive top of society to the common bottom.

Human justice must be taught and practiced in every home. Fair play must be learned in the kindergarten. It must be practiced and taught in the schools. The institutions of higher education must extol the benefits of justice. If students are required to learn to balance equations in mathematics, they must not neglect to learn how to balance equations in human relationships and social interactions. What does it profit a student to be academically accurate and morally and mentally unbalanced?

Human justice must be commonplace in business. Injustice must not be tolerated in the workplace. The government ought to be the symbol and the shining example of human justice for all the people. The churches and religious institutions, with their creeds of benevolence and goodwill, must go beyond justice. They must be the vanguard in implementing and putting into practice the theory of love. The church must take the leadership in transforming the creeds into deeds. The church must lift up its voice and trumpet into the ears of the people the requirements and the benefits of justice. It must also warn of the destructive consequences of injustice. The goal of the church and the prayer of the church must be that God's will be done on earth as it is in heaven.

The halls of criminal justice and the chambers of civil justice must be sacred. It must be a place where fairness prevails and human rights are guaranteed. It must be a place where justice is the first and second priority. It must be a place where justice is tempered with mercy. It must be a place where the common people can look to with respect, trust and hope. It must be a place of esteem and honor.

Those who administer justice must accept their responsibility with the seriousness of a brain surgeon or heart specialist. The administration of justice requires the highest professional competency and the most humane sensitivity available. For those who administer justice, deal with the most sacred of human values. They deal with human rights, freedom, life, liberty, the pursuit of happiness, and even death. Therefore, those who administer justice must have clear minds, clean hearts and a right spirit. Those who have accepted the awesome responsibility of administering justice are not only accountable to the government and the people, but they are also accountable to God.

## THE WAYS OF JUSTICE

The ways of justice are divine and eternal. Justice is a condition created by God to maintain balance in the human enterprise. It is desirable and achievable by the righteous and conscientious efforts of people of goodwill. It is the natural way. It is the way of nature and the universe. It is the logical way. Justice makes sense. It is scientific, but not limited to science. Many aspects of justice are measurable. It suggests evenness and equality. The complexities of human involvement and human behavior frequently rule out simplistic decisions. Therefore, the process of arriving at justice in many instances can be as intricate as problems in biochemistry or physics. And that is why it is mandatory, that those who are in positions to administer justice, must be capable of understanding and dealing effectively with the intricacies of legal mathematics, social chemistry and political physics.

The way of human justice is the democratic way. Its power is derived from the consent of the governed. Its final authority is from God. Justice is the constructive way. It minimizes friction, increases balance and enhances stability in society. Justice increases cohesion and solidarity among the members of the society. Justice is the human way. It is the way of enlightened civilization. It represents cultural and social refinement. Human justice is the way of righteousness. Righteousness is the way of God. It represents the deep yearning of the human spirit for unity, peace and the brotherhood and sisterhood of all human beings.

## A PLEA FOR SOCIAL JUSTICE

Let Justice make straight the crooked places.
Let it visit the needy and exalt their low estate.
Let it lighten the burdens of the homeless and needy.
Let justice free the poor from the shackles of their oppression.

Let justice bring relief to the victims of crime.
Let it vindicate those who are falsely accused.
Let it bring relief to the deprived and despairing.
Let justice make whole the tortured and injured.

Let justice prevail throughout this land,
Let it prevail in the White House, the Courthouse and the State House.
Let it prevail on the land and all the Islands.
Let it prevail in the seas, on the oceans and the outreaches of space.
Let the wheels of justice turn in the criminal courts.
Let them turn in the civil courts, traffic and magistrate courts. Let the wheels of justice turn in the Justice Department.

Let the wheels of justice turn in the jails, bureau of police and correctional institutions.

Let justice speak from the councils of municipal government. Let it speak from the corporate boardrooms and government bureaucracies.
Let justice rule with the strong arms of righteousness.
Let it judge with the clean hands of equality.
Let justice speak with the clear voice of freedom.
Let justice do its sacred work with compassion.

Let the trumpets of justice sound from the pulpits.
Let the drums of justice beat in the streets, athletic, and entertainment halls.

Let justice rule in every home, on the playground and neighborhoods.
Let justice be the rule and the policy in the workplace.
Let it govern from executive suites to maintenance closets.

Let justice absorb education from kindergarten through high school.
Let it obsess the halls of academia and all institutions of learning.

Let justice reign in America, in every city and township.
Let it reign in every county, every reservation, district and province.
Let it reign! Reign! Reign!
Let justice prevail in every country and throughout the earth! Let only justice speak for the people!
Let only justice sit on the throne!